# T. F. POWYS

T. F. Powys at Mappowder, Aged Sixty Seven

# T. F. POWYS

*By*

## H. COOMBES

LONDON
BARRIE AND ROCKLIFF

MADE AND PRINTED IN GREAT BRITAIN BY
BURLEIGH LIMITED AT THE BURLEIGH PRESS
BRISTOL

# CONTENTS

But man, proud man!
Dress'd in a little brief authority,
Most ignorant of what he's most assured
(His glassy essence), like an angry ape,
Plays such fantastic tricks before high heaven
As make the angels weep; who with our spleens,
Would all themselves laugh mortal.
*Measure for Measure.*


Dost thou think, because thou art virtuous,
that there shall be no more cakes and ale?
*Twelfth Night.*


Lie thee down, Oddity!
T. F. POWYS.

*Chapter One*

# INTRODUCTORY

ROUGHLY half-way along the road from Dorchester to Wareham there is a signpost bearing the name of East Chaldon. The lane takes you south towards the Dorset coast with its white cliffs and pebbly beaches and dark rocks rising from the sea, which on sunny days is hereabouts marvellously blue. Chaldon is within two or three miles of the Lulworths and the striking rock-formation known as the Durdle Door. The sea is not visible from the village, which is almost encircled with grassy hills. As you were approaching Chaldon you would probably pause at the bend where the village comes suddenly and beautifully into view. This would be the place where Mr. Weston stopped his Ford car before going about his business in the village of Folly Down. For it was at East Chaldon that T. F. Powys did almost all his writing, including the great novelistic allegory, *Mr. Weston's Good Wine*. A dozen or so miles to the north is the tiny village of Mappowder, and it is here that Powys is buried. Nearly all his adult life was lived in these two remote villages.

The sun and the grave are consistently present in the writings of Theodore Powys, both in their physical being and symbolically. He can be said to exemplify and to give an intensely

7

individual meaning to the truism that the great themes of art
are life and death. The sun and what we associate with it of
happiness and pleasure, the grave and what it suggests of
solemnity, horror and grief, these are realities in his mind and
in his work. A further great reality is his vision of death in the
sun and life in the grave.

It may be thought, in the absence here of more explanation,
that such a vision belongs to that mystical-paradoxical kind
that tends to be too common. But in using the words at this
juncture I wish to do no more than hint at an important
element of the contemplation which lies behind the writings,
in particular the superb fables and short stories and the two
finest novels. Powys had that rarest of capacities, not to be self-
deceived, involving both a penetration of the appearances of
everyday life and a profound pondering on death. The sort of
discipline entailed in the belief that truth matters enabled him
to see and to accept steadily many things which people do
not normally see, or if seeing turn away from or disguise with
a mask.

It may seem surprising to speak of acceptance in connection
with a man whose sufferings and strains are so often apparent
in his writing and who moreover characteristically employed
non-realistic modes of expression. But it is precisely through
these modes that we have the opportunity of an enriching
contact with poise and firmness based upon a spiritual and
sensuous responsiveness quietly alert and deep. And with the
life of the senses and mind and spirit goes a strong and tender
care for the details of day-to-day living: the cats about the
house, the wood to be chopped in the garden shed, the mush-
rooms that he liked to bring in from the fields for supper, were
accounted by him to be as surely a part of life as writing books
and reading Jane Austen or Freud or the Bible or Rabelais.

This book is written in the belief that T. F. Powys is an
original genius, one of the great writers of the twentieth
century. To speak of greatness and originality is to suggest the
range and quality of the experience that he is master of, and

the importance of his themes and interests, and the force and beauty of his presentation. Ultimately it is where the force and beauty lie, in other words technique as the expression of vision and character, that is our justification for claiming such a range and such an importance. For clearly the range is not social or topographical: it would be hard to find a life more free from exciting external events than that of T. F. Powys. But so deep is his understanding within his chosen field, so sure the touch with which he handles his themes of permanent significance, that no writer is less provincial. His best work prompts us to speak of wisdom.

Theodore Francis Powys was the third of a family of eleven children. Of these one died in youth; almost all the others survived into old age; at the moment of writing five are living. It is of course a family famous for the mark made by several of its members in our time. Besides the writers John Cowper Powys (living) and Llewelyn and Theodore, there are Gertrude who was a painter of some note, A. R. Powys an admirable architect who was for many years Secretary of the Society for the Preservation of Ancient Buildings, Marian (living) a leading authority on lace in the United States, William (living) a noted farmer in Africa; Littleton, the most conventional of the family, was well known in local circles, academic, sporting, and civic; Catherine Philippa and Lucy, the two youngest daughters, live country-loving lives in the south of England.

It is hardly necessary here to do more than mention that the Powys ancestry flows from little-known late-medieval sources through eighteenth century landed proprietors and lawyers and clerics down to Charles Francis Powys (born 1843), clergyman and father of the celebrated family. Some information has been provided in autobiographical and kindred books by the recognised writers of the family, and in works by Louis Wilkinson ('Marlow': *Welsh Ambassadors*, Chapman and Hall, 1936, and *Seven Friends*, Richards Press, 1953), Malcolm Elwin (*Life of Llewelyn Powys*, The Bodley Head, 1946), Richard Heron Ward (*The Powys Brothers*, The Bodley Head, 1936). More fact and interpretation may be found in a pamphlet entitled *The Powys Family*, by Littleton Powys, and an article, 'The Quiet Man of Dorset', by T. F.'s son Francis, published in *The Adelphi*, Fourth Quarter, 1954. 'A Famous Family', by Alyse Gregory, widow of Llewelyn, appeared in *The London Magazine* for March, 1958.

It is outside my purpose to attempt any generalisation about the family except in so far as it may help in the fuller revelation of Theodore. Accounts of parents by their children and of families by members of them are evidence to be handled delicately, and when a strict evangelical clergyman with eleven children and a dutiful and loving wife who became 'resigned' are a subject of enquiry, then we shall do well to proceed with caution. But perhaps one thing may at this point be usefully said: nearly all the children dropped their father's piety. Their individualism often took the form of conscious rebellion against orthodoxy of belief and behaviour, and Marian, crippled with arthritis, crossing the Atlantic and going the rounds at seventy-seven years old, and William tending and watching animals and painting landscapes on his Kenya farm, are no less individualists than John Cowper with his ardent pantheism and Llewelyn the atheist with his lyrical insistence on seizing the moment. Theodore's revolt shaped itself into subtle directions. It is interesting that he, the quietest person of them all and the quietest writer, incurred more general opposition than any of them. He is of course what we are apt to call enigmatic. Mr. Norman Nicholson has characterised him (along with Joyce) as 'bawdy and blasphemous'; yet only recently I received a letter from someone who was well acquainted with him, rather anxiously assuring me that T. F. Powys was not at all of the 'early fleshly' school but was a most devout believer and church-goer.

Powys was born in 1875 at Shirley in Derbyshire, where his father was Vicar. In 1879 a move was made, with the first five children, to Dorchester, and six years later, with three more children, to Montacute in Somerset. It is Montacute with which the Rev. C. F. Powys is mainly associated. He was Vicar here for thirty years. And here Theodore with his numerous brothers and sisters shared the life of comparative opulence which his father's considerable means provided. Religious duties in the house were many and frequent, but the children made full use also of the rich countryside, the orchards, hills, fields, gardens. The father was himself a great walker and encouraged an interest in nature. Theodore, even in these boyhood days, was fond of making off alone; he had a hide-out in the garden, made by himself, and called 'Bushes Home'.

Unlike his two senior brothers Theodore did not go to Cambridge. He was educated first at Dorchester Grammar School, then at Sherborne, and finally at Aldeburgh, where he met Louis Wilkinson (son of the proprietor of the school) who was to remain his friend for more than sixty years.

On finishing school he decided to go in for farming, and after a short training period his father bought him a farm at Sweffling in Suffolk. Apparently he was not a bad farmer, but he did not care enough for the work to stay in it, and after four or five years he moved back to Dorset to live with all the quiet he could find, and to write. Louis Wilkinson tells how as an undergraduate he frequently stayed with Theodore at Sweffling, the topics of conversation including Nietzsche, Schopenhauer, Swinburne and other poets, Leslie Stephen, Cotter Morrison 'and other Rationalist writers of the day'. In his article for *The Aylesford Review*, Mr. Wilkinson goes on to say: 'Far more important to me than any books in throwing light on a new world was Theodore himself, not only his words but his presence. "In the presence" was what I felt when I was with him.' A sense of power in reserve was at the centre of the impression which many people received of Powys's personality.

Back in Dorset, he lived for a short while at the seaside village of Studland before moving to East Chaldon in 1904. He was to live here for some thirty-seven years, most of the time at 'Beth Car', the House in the Field. In 1905 he married Violet Rosalie Dodd. It was shortly before this that he had begun to write. Possibly the death (in distressing circumstances) of his elder son, in Kenya in 1931, had something to do with his virtually ceasing to write at about that time. A baby girl, Susan, was adopted in 1933.

Though it was the remoteness of Chaldon that took Powys there and kept him there with his family for so many years, he was not a hermit in the usual sense of the word. Apart from his love of walking—'Madder Hill' is across the road—visits from relations and friends were frequent. Two of his sisters and Llewelyn and his wife lived close by. When John Cowper or William or Bertie (A. R.) came there were long walks and long talks and there were often convivial meetings at the year's end. For holidays there was Montacute, where the ageing parents, but especially the father, must have looked with very mixed feelings on the son who was idling his life away in obscurity. Through all this life Violet was never wanting with her love, her shrewd practicality and not least her candour and down-rightness, qualities much valued by T. F. Powys.

In 1939 illness came, and the following year, amid the din of air-battle, he was moved northwards a dozen miles to Mappowder. He recovered a fair degree of health, but by now his writing-days were as good as over. Between 1932 and his death in 1953 his only publications of any size were the two collections of short stories, *Captain Patch* (1935) and *Bottle's Path* (1946). He had to nurse his health. His home life, his books, his short walks, his meditation, his talks with a few friends, were all he wanted.

Among the friends and admirers (excluding relatives) of T. F. Powys—and it may be said here that the names of this paragraph are not offered as comprising an exhaustive list— Louis Wilkinson is prominent not only by virtue of his long personal friendship but also by his having contended always for the pre-eminence of Theodore among the writer-brothers. Harold Raymond, then of Chatto and Windus, was a great friend who gave much kindly advice and encouragement, and the same may be said of Charles Prentice, also of Chatto's.

Another who helped with discussion and criticism of T. F.'s work and who introduced it to other people was Stephen Tomlin, the sculptor. Douglas Goldring also was an early 'champion': it was he who recommended Knopf to publish *The Left Leg* and *Black Bryony* in America. Other writers whom he knew and (in varying degrees) was companionable with included Hardy, Sylvia Townsend Warner (with whom he had much talk and to one of whose books he contributed the only preface he ever wrote), David Garnett, Gerald Brenan, Valentine Acland, William Hunter. Dr. Bernard Price O'Neill was a very close friend of T. F., as he was of all the Powyses. An occasional visitor to Beth Car was T. E. Lawrence. Augustus John, in a letter to Mrs. Violet Powys about his portrait of T. F. (begun many years ago but because of damage put aside, then finally appearing in the Academy in 1958), wrote: ' I shall never forget Theodore Powys.' F. R. Leavis wrote on Powys at a time (the late 'twenties) when he was doing his pioneering work on Lawrence and Eliot; he visited Powys at Beth Car.

Powys's life, then, despite these relatives and acquaintances, was spent away from 'the world'. He sought the country always and deliberately; he left his village only when he had to and only for the shortest possible length of time. The small journey to Weymouth or Dorchester he found tiresome: ' . . . this cursed getting up early to catch the carrier—he goes to Dorchester—is unpleasant', is one of many similar remarks in letters published by Louis Wilkinson in *Welsh Ambassadors*.

Powys knew what material poverty was; he was poor for a long time after leaving the comfortable family home. He seems to have decided to write soon after the turn of the century, and thereafter for many years he and his family existed on an allowance from his father of something between one and two pounds a week. Llewelyn writes of the shock he had when on one occasion he met Theodore who was out at heels and knees and elbows. Theodore did not mind on his own account, but there were times when he was worried and depressed about the

welfare of his family. It was not until 1923, when he was
forty-eight, that he became 'known' with the publication of
*The Left Leg*. From then on until the early 'thirties his novels
and stories appeared regularly. Among much adverse comment
there were perceptive and encouraging reviews, but most of
the books sold in very small quantities. Later in life he was
somewhat better off, being helped considerably by a Civil List
pension.

Perhaps it is inevitable that those who knew T. F. Powys in
life should offer widely diverse impressions of him, while
agreeing on certain basic features of his character. Interpretation largely remains as always a matter of where we put our
emphasis. When one has gathered the outward facts—the
middling-tall height, the changing expressiveness of the grey-
blue eyes, the lips inclined to shut tight, the low and musical
and rather slow voice, the complete lack of demonstrativeness
and gesturing—there is left the complex personality. Francis
Powys has told me that for him the salient feature of his father's
conversation was wit, a wit fantastic or profound, often fantastic
and profound together, and always offered quietly for amusement and as comment. Alyse Gregory has stressed his fondness
for 'homely' subjects in talk, while saying also that 'Almost his
every word contained something of the unexpected'. Louis
Wilkinson calls him 'a born mystic with his own heterodox
mysticism'. Confessions and manifestoes are not always as
enlightening as they claim to be, but in the case of Powys, with
no wilful misleading and about as little self-deception as a
human being can have, there are certain things in *Soliloquies
of a Hermit* (which he revised for re-publication when he was
well advanced into his forties) which admirably present and
illuminate some important aspects of the man and his everyday
life.

He is quite aware of the contradictions in the *Soliloquies*:
' . . . sometimes I appear to be an infidel and sometimes a
believer, sometimes a Christian and sometimes a heathen, and
every brave man is just the same as I am.' He knows what

struggle is involved in facing and uttering one's hidden side :
> In speaking or writing a confession, one is always
> coming near to something ugly in the dark of oneself.
> I touch the hoof, or the fur, or the horns, or the tusks,
> as I write.

But the contradictions and the struggle do not prevent the clear
emergence of a central feature: the co-existence of contemplation with a rare esteem for the commonplace in day-to-day
living.

> No doubt one day we shall find all the mystic writers
> leaving their pens and their burrowings into the un-
> utterable mystery of God's being, and instead busying
> themselves all day long peacefully planting cabbages.

This is of course a simple playful hope, perhaps even a sort of
encouragement to himself for having escaped from, in his own
words, 'the old days' when 'I used to tie myself up in a mystic
knot'. But the book in its entirety makes it quite clear that his
mystic searchings, his sometimes Jefferies-like declarations—

> I wish to drink deep of the silence, the deep mists, the
> growing corn, and the movements of birds. The very life
> that I feel around me should drug me, and each motion
> and movement and tongue of fire that I feel ought
> to pass like rich wine into my being. The very stones
> of the road should yield up to me their thoughts.

—are consonant with this:

> I have never had the least objection to ugly things.
> If my fire warms me, what do I care if the grate is a
> square black hole in the wall, with three varnished
> iron sunflowers in a row above it ?

and with his claim to the right to be unconventional in his
simplicity-in-idleness:

> I pray that I may always be allowed to keep my blood
> cool by watching the cows and by moving brown earth
> under the sun. Must everyone here on earth be either
> ordering or obeying, stealing or giving, blessing or
> cursing ?

The kind of people that I find most unpleasant to my taste, are the people that look and smile and walk on. These are they that find fault;—the fault-finders, the people that point at your thistles and count your nettles, that wonder why you do not keep fowls, or why you keep a row of five broken buckets by your back door . . .

It has taken long enough to make a man, and now a man sits in disgrace and hates himself because in one day he has done nothing. What after all are the very wonderful doings of man worth? Very likely by doing nothing we may be going a little way on the right road, and by doing a great deal we may only be going round the same old way again, the same old way that leads to common rows of houses, municipal buildings, and petrol-filled machines.

But the so-called simple life, he claims, is the deeper life. The really simple life is the life of cars, divorces, dances, hunting, shooting, competitive games. The pleasures of that life are not like the joy to be won from his own:

I want to cultivate the kind of mind that can turn stones into bread, a dull hour into heavenly glory, and a dull life into the life of a king. For what we call dullness is really the best soil we can dig in, because the gold that it yields is very precious and very lasting. I like to know that I am getting rich, not by stealing from the poor, but by getting something more out of myself; I want to get all I can out of myself, and what I want to get is the thing that shall please me.

Once past the first page or two, which seem rather determinedly paradoxical, the *Soliloquies* offers a notable statement of a position and an attitude as well as an impression of Powys hoeing his garden and mending his railings.

In his article, 'The Quiet Man of Dorset', Francis Powys stresses the steady regularity of his father's writing-habits: he wrote and revised a little every morning. Mr. Powys has this to say also about the manner and progress of T.F.'s work and publication: 'For many years, publishers and editors would have none of him and Theodore worked on without recognition. His cupboards became filled with manuscripts copied and re-copied laboriously in longhand. When finally he became known his books were published in quick succession, for he only needed to open one of those cupboards to produce a ready-made novel or a short story.'

These circumstances make it difficult to be sure about an exact order of composition of Powys's works, but fortunately we have a certain amount of information (see Bibliography) which tallies with the deductions we might make from internal evidence. *The Left Leg* and *Hester Dominy* appeared together in the same volume in 1923, but it is clear that the finer vision and maturer viewpoint of the former go also with a more practised hand in writing. Similarly we should not have to depend upon a knowledge of dates to know that *Mark Only* is a more accom-plished piece of work than *Black Bryony*. An attempt to determine an exact order of writing for all the works would have to fail, if only because of the overlapping that occurs with revisions and rewritings. But we know enough to give us (as subsequent chapters will help to show) the picture of a develop-ment in which certain crudities and over-insistencies are discarded and outgrown in the progress towards the experience represented by the summit achievements. I think we shall do well, however, not to allow our value-judgments to make us unduly exclusive. Many of even the markedly inferior things have something that is likely to interest anyone who recognises Powys as the great author of *Mr. Weston* and *Fables*.

The question arises here of precisely that recognition. Why should it be, we may ask, without any reflection on John Cowper and Llewelyn, that they are much more often to be found on the library shelves than T.F.? *Mr. Weston's Good Wine* has been widely read and has been reprinted many times since it appeared first in 1927. But it seems to get little attention for the living classic it undoubtedly is. Even the great and

B

fascinating *Fables* seem little known, and despite the appearance
from time to time of appreciative notices and articles and even
sections of books, one feels perfectly justified in speaking of
Powys as a neglected genius.

It is not surprising that a writer who so unremittingly
confined himself to rural settings and (with a few very important
exceptions) to rural types, should come under fire from one
direction or another. But even when to that restriction—
which is deliberately self-imposed for particular ends—is
added the disturbingly individual treatment and technique,
there can be no possible case for the sort of judgment that is
contained in the following:

> Everyone, in this sophisticatedly contrived bucolic
> morality, has his or her obsession: Minnie Wurzel
> wants only the vicar; the vicar the Reverend Nut,
> wants only the ghost of William Cowper to come into
> his brown study and read him 'The Task'; the sexton
> wants the worms; worms want the vicar. Lambkins, on
> those impossible hills, frolic, gambol, and are
> sheepish under the all-seeing eye of Uncle Teapot, the
> Celestial Tinker. Cruel farmers persecute old cowherds
> called Crumpet, who talk, all day long, to cows;
> cows, tired of vaccine-talk in which they can have no
> part, gore, in a female manner, the aged relatives
> of cruel farmers . . .

The most charitable thing that can be said about remarks like
these—they were made by Dylan Thomas in a broadcast and
they are perpetuated in *Quite Early One Morning*—is that they
issue simply from lack of knowledge and of experience in both
life and literature. That the author of *Under Milk Wood* should
charge T. F. Powys with contributing to the rustic myth of
bizarre and morbid and sinister passions—Mary Webb, and
Stella Gibbons's burlesque, *Cold Comfort Farm*, were contemporary with Powys—provides a neat example of self-ignorance.
Much the same misrepresentation was made, though lacking
facetiousness, by Richard Heron Ward when in *The Powys*

*Brothers* he expatiated upon T. F.'s 'corrupt and evil pre-occupation with sex, a preoccupation amounting to nothing less than a mania', and upon his 'peculiarly ugly sadism'.

The case of Powys, were it known as widely, would be hardly less instructive than that of Lawrence in the matter of right appreciation and public attitudes. He is, of course, a challenge to facile and illusory thinking; he questions (though for the most part implicitly) the assumptions and sanctions which underlie and govern our civilisation. But this alone would hardly account for lack of recognition. Nor, in the twentieth century, would his frankness and sometimes violence when he is dealing with sex. Some readers may find his insistence on the fact of death unpleasant; some find his treatment of 'God' blasphemous; some may consider him too moralistic. But while these may be adequate reasons for a lack of wide popularity they do not explain the comparative meagreness of recognition by advanced opinion. Perhaps the two main causes are these: a failure to see that his 'narrow' rural world is a perfectly adequate basis for the expression of a whole attitude to life, and the consequent or allied failure to appreciate the nature of his conventions. Simply, Powys is a great and an extraordinary writer. He has, to adapt T. S. Eliot's words about Blake, 'the terrifying honesty of genius'. Much of our task lies in coming to see that what may at first seem 'terrifying' is in reality healthy and nourishing.

It is interesting to ponder that a man who read the lessons for nearly forty years in a village church can be seen as a virulent hater of God and religion; that a passage like this :

> He looked at the Madder valley. The great elms were crowned with gold, the red and white cows lay peacefully where the soft haze warmed the meadows and Madder Hill waited, with the grace of a lonely and lovely virgin, for God's gift to come.

comes from the pen of the writer who moves Mr. Ward to cry out in protest, 'This terrible God, this pagan and uncivilised and Judaic God, stalks through the pages of Theodore Powys's books as He stalks through the heart of their writer.'

This is intended to be a powerfully damaging judgment. Actually the impression it gives of Powys is ludicrously erroneous. I wonder just what his feelings were when he first read this about himself, he the creator of Mr. Weston, John Death, Tinker or Squire Jar, Mr. Pim, Mr. Cronch, and many more? And that word 'stalks', how could anyone use it who had approached either the writings or the man with full attention and with an open mind? Nothing 'stalks' in T. F. Powys. However, an appreciation of Powys that would account itself complete is by no means easy to achieve. Issues are often delicate and pitfalls are many.

The care that is needed to reveal and interpret Powys is not least when 'influences' are under discussion. He grew into independence at an early age, and the way of life he chose was maintained steadily in face of the difficulties which are the usual lot of the writer who works both geographically and otherwise at a distance from the centre of the literary world. He was moreover without pusillanimity in breaking the great herd-law of 'Thou shalt work hard for the good of this our society', as he was without expectation of society's approval and rewards. Glad when the critics and reviewers spoke well of his work, his happiness did not in the slightest depend upon praise. He commanded his life.

Psychologists and others who have read Powys might be able to point with some confidence to places where there was between-the-lines evidence of his descent from a line of clerical ancestors; they might discuss profitably his father and mother, and perhaps more profitably still the relationship between them; they might even suggest inheritances from his forbear William Cowper and his possible forbear John Donne; they could talk of Powys with Freud and Nietzsche and Rabelais as prompters (all of whom we know he was well acquainted with). Literary critics and general readers will at times adduce the Bible, Bunyan, Jane Austen as potent presences. But the presences are only contributory to the main force. Powys, like all true artists, was an individual in the deep sense: influences joined and merged in the creation of a strongly living man, the mature man who is the master and whom no influence can be said to dominate. And as we cannot, without important qualifications, speak usefully of influences on T. F. Powys, so we cannot speak to any useful purpose of the consequences for his art of his day-to-day living. It was not his country-and-domestic life that dictated his themes and conditioned his treatment of them; he chose that life deliberately and with full knowledge. It was a good life for him and for his wife and children, and the way of it enabled him to write his books.

In the course of an article about his house and garden, written in that phase of his life when, as he put it, 'the tide is at the ebb', Powys had this to say :

> I hate the dainty cottage of modern nicety; the build
> of ours is far more to my mind. One is supposed to
> sigh, as though one should worship, when the door
> is opened and one beholds a jade carving. I would
> prefer to see a black bottle, that a poor man may at
> least become better acquainted with.

And a little later:

> If you look for sweet-williams beside our door, you will
> only find bindweed, and in the garden you will only
> see haycocks where there should be potatoes.

Untidiness? indifference? weariness even? It hardly matters, for the corollary of that sort of un-care, which was habitual with him, was a profound care for his writing, with its suffering and its enjoyments, its violences and horrors and its beautiful quiet places, its bitterness, its humour and its ironies, its true solemnities.

*Chapter Two*

# THE EARLIER NOVELS

EXCLUSIVE of *Mr. Weston* and *Unclay* there are six full-length novels by Powys, and six short ones. As these works are comparatively little known it will not be superfluous to offer the informing idea behind each or the main thread of the action. The works are given in the order of publication, the short ones being asterisked:

*The Left Leg\*:* greed and lust ending in self-destruction.

*Hester Dominy\*:* a young woman escapes from a drab and monotonous life in the town only to find that for her the country is equally drab and monotonous.

*Abraham Men\*:* the unsuccessful attempt of a brewery clerk turned evangelist to move the 'sluggish mass' of the people of Dodder village.

*Black Bryony:* a Salvation Army girl alternating between a most exalted evangelism and the fulfilling of a passionate sensual nature.

*Mark Only:* the failure in love and life of a ploughman of extremely limited mind and capacities.

*Mr. Tasker's Gods:* conflict between the mild and unambitious and gently 'good', on the one hand, and on the other the worldly and ostentatious and hypocritical.

*Mockery Gap:* irrational frustrating fears in the lives of several people; unfulfilment; liberations brought about by 'the fisherman'.

*Innocent Birds:* the powerlessness of the 'innocents' to withstand the antagonistic malice of the vicious.

*Kindness in a Corner:* the Rev. Dottery's mellow life but without a woman's love; the kind corners are several; Mr. Dottery's home and work, the village of Tadnol, the sexual 'corner', the corner that is the grave.

*In Good Earth\*:* a passionate-natured young man's search for a satisfying channel for his energies.

*God\*:* a small boy seeks and eventually finds a quite unconventional 'God'.

*The Two Thieves\*:* a man drinks of the vials (stolen from the Devil) of Greed, Anger, Pride, and Cruelty. In the end he is himself robbed and punished by 'Mr. Jar'.

Those readers who are not acquainted with the works given here will do well not to draw any but the most tentative conclusions from the abstractions offered: the ideas and the happenings have their meaning only in the unique world of Powys's writings.

The world of Theodore Powys is Dorset, and it is the human spirit. All goes on

'as one views a picture', thought Solly, 'a picture that can show a vaster and a grander one behind it.'

(*Innocent Birds*)

The surface of rural life, the activities seen and heard and understood, the wealth of natural things to be sensuously enjoyed, are always present. But he sees too, and with an extraordinary power, the movements behind and beneath; he is aware always of the cycle of life, death, birth, life, death. His delineation of the everyday carries with it a portrayal of the deep-down human desires, passionate drives, conflicts. The carter, the parson, the innkeeper, the servant girl, have more to do than busy themselves with horses, sermons, glasses, and brooms; life doesn't let them off so easily; they have the dark underworld of emotion to contend with, even though they may not be consciously aware of it. Nevertheless the day-to-day actualities of the world in which they are presented are an integral part of Powys's work, and we shall see how quick and spontaneous is his appraisal of the rich usefulness for his purpose of this or that rural scene or detail.

The *dramatis personae* of this stage can be readily suggested in simple broad terms: clergymen, sometimes naïve and good, sometimes learned and kindly, sometimes selfish, hard and hypocritical; farmers avaricious and cruel, and less often, farmers and husbandmen quietly content in their vocation; 'merry maidens'; sextons; parasitic and mischievous ne'er-do-wells; likeable idlers; snobbish ladies; over-worked servants; gossipers; village 'innocents'; innkeepers. In addition to these —the list is not complete—there are the 'supernatural' figures. Mr. Jar for instance, and the fisherman in *Mockery Gap*, and John Death, and Mr. Weston himself: these haunting characters are often used by Powys for his deepest purposes and with wonderful effect. Jar appears in many stories; so do several of the ordinary village inhabitants: Pring the road-mender, Miss Pettifer the superior, self-righteous lady, Mr. Balliboy the carrier, sexton Truggin, Lord Bullman, and others.

Superficially the people of the novels seem unexciting and commonplace enough, apart from the 'Jar' group. But it is precisely Powys's intention to present the 'commonplace'; his village is the world, and its men and women exemplify the ruling dispositions and passions of mankind: from comprehensive egoism, greed, sadism physical and mental, malice, possessive lust, and so on, to kindliness, generosity, sympathy, love. When Powys is in full control of his material he is with the great writers of the language. When his success is partial we shall probably find that it is either on account of some unmastered inward stress which turns the vision too much one way, or because of a failure to use artistically a propensity towards fancifulness and whimsy. In *Mr. Weston*, in much of *Unclay*, in *Fables* and other stories, this propensity becomes a virtue because it is emotionally charged and profoundly integrated in the whole.

The title story of Powys's first published volume of stories, *The Left Leg*, is, within its limits, extremely fine. It was certainly a 'new voice' (as several reviewers stated but mostly failed to substantiate), new both by virtue of the nature and intensity of the preoccupations revealed and by the way in which they are communicated. The theme of *The Left Leg* is lust for possessions animate and inanimate, a lust accompanied with restlessness and rage and ending in self-destruction. It is rendered with a force and a poetic suggestiveness which( this being his habitual way) put Powys among those novelists whom F. R. Leavis more than anyone has accustomed us to think of as in large measure 'dramatic poets'.

The principal characters are Farmer Mew, whose 'habit of life was to clutch all'; Farmer James Gillet, growing poorer and poorer as he seeks the meaning of life in prayer; Mary, Gillet's daughter; Minnie Cuddy, a kind-hearted easy widow who lives in Love Cottage; Mad Tom Button, who never lets us forget Mr. Jar and who is always eagerly expectant of his return to the village of God's Madder; and Mr. Jar himself, absent from Madder for most of the duration of the action but returning to be the saviour of Mary when, with child by Mew, she attempts to drown herself, and then as the agent of retribution for Mew's whole way of life. Several subsidiary characters help to subtilise and enrich.

The force and suggestiveness of the story, which is Powysian in the convincing reality of its part-naturalistic part-fantastic world, derive from several interrelated things: the power of the narrative at certain moments, the intensity with which Mew is portrayed in his aims and lusts and rages, the sense of coming retribution. The character of Mew recalls traditional symbolic characters like Chaucer's Pardoner, and Volpone, and Mr. Pecksniff. For it is not only the irony of prefacing and concluding such a grim uncompromising story—Mew's left leg falls from the sky when he blows himself up—with the nursery rhyme about the old man who would not say his prayers, that gives the story 'comic' horror.

Farmer Mew is relentless in his greed and inhumanity:

> He now nearly possessed the whole village. By degrees, by little and little, he had clutched near all there was to be had. It was said in Madder that if Mr. Mew looked at anything, whether sheep, oxen, house or land, he could charm the thing to be his.
>
> 'Farmer do swallow all,' Mother Button said.
>
> One day Farmer Mew saw Mary Gillet in her garden. Only the day before he had seen a hundred young ewes at market and had bought them.
>
> Farmer Mew was unmarried.
>
> If he saw a blackbird on a hedge and wished for it he would get his gun, and very soon the bird would be in his hand.
>
> He now wanted Mary.
>
> Mr. Mew was tall, he had a broad back, and a hand that clutched. His eyes were grey and his look dark and gloomy. Mad Button would run away when he saw Mr. Mew in the lane.

We do not feel that second 'clutched' merely as a repetition of the idea of greed; we connect it with Mary: other girls have been used by him. It is because we are made to see the monstrous folly that accompanied monstrous egoism that Mew becomes for us a caricature, savagely comic. In emulation of a flower-gathering girl he gathers armfuls himself, but tramples on them in rage when he sees the field is just as yellow as it was before; he takes butterflies from a boy and hits with his stick at others flying; he hammers in vain at Jar's Stone; he has a shockingly violent death. But with this tinct of caricature goes, on occasions, something which brings us a sense almost of admiration at the 'richness' of his vice: in the scene where Mew is driving a stolen flock of sheep along the lane in the moonlight he is like Volpone, or the Jew of Malta, gloating imaginatively over his wealth. The episode is given with a full sensuous evocativeness: we feel the immense joy and elation with which Mew hears the music of the rumble of the many feet, and smells the hot soft scent, and exults in the thick mat of wool made by the crowded backs. We feel, too, the stealth of the act: all the time, behind the immediately perceived, his doom is preparing.

Happenings in nature are used for atmosphere and as signs. The wind behaves strangely on what is 'just a usual autumn evening':

> Wild gusts beat upon the bare Madder trees, and the sound of the wind was like the sound of heavy footfalls.

And later:

> The wind blew again in wild beating gusts—like the beating of huge wings upon the roof of heaven, or deep steps in the sky.
> Someone in the village was calling.

These passages take on a still deeper note if we recall the night when, before her 'destruction', Mary asked her father if Mr. Mew was a good man, and on receiving no answer expressed the wish that Mr. Jar would come back; after she got home she looked from her bedroom into the still summer night:

> Outside in the road she heard the heavy footsteps of a man who seemed to be striding up and down.

Those were Mew's footsteps. The wind's gusts portend the return of Jar. In a most impressive chapter (XXI) in which most of the characters of the drama appear, we are given that return and the struggle with Mew. It is while Mr. Jar is going with Minnie Cuddy to Mew's house that Mad Button's voice is heard calling by the Madder well:

> 'Wold Jar be come, wold Jar be come,' the voice called.
> 'Who be wold Jar?' the voice asked itself.
> ''E be the leaf that do drift in the wind. 'E be the cloud that do cross the moon at night-time. 'E be the stone that a poor man do take up in road to throw at his dog. 'E be the pond weeds where do bide the wold toad. 'E be the bastard child before 'tis born. Wold Jar be come.'

The quality and organisation of the language here is *poetic* in
its deep rhythms and its surface music and by virtue of the fact
that almost all the identifications of Jar as given by Mad Tom
recall unmistakably scenes or things or events that have gone
before. Poetic, in fact, is Powys's method throughout: there are
many symbols, images, juxtapositions. Minnie Cuddy's general
liberality is suggested in a sentence like: 'Mrs. Minnie Cuddy
threw out handfuls of golden maize to her hens'; and we feel the
implied contrast with Mew who grasps all to him. The powerful
scene where Jar opposes Mew—Mew 'stood as though he were
resisting to the uttermost a huge force. With every sinew he
fought Jar'—is given through the eyes of Tom, who is crouched
on Jar's Stone outside the window; the scene has the moving
and mysterious effect of dumb show. Then there are the
Summerbees; the inadequacy of their view of life—and they are
a 'pleasant' couple who mean well—is suggested in many
touches:

> To Mr. Summerbee Madder was only a pretty plate
> that held Susan. Madder was the plate and Susan the
> strawberry. Other figures decorated the plate too.

To the right hand of Madder, in a field where there is a tiny
spot of red, the bull that has gored Mrs. Patch is pawing the
ground and tossing up earth with its horns; to the left hand,
Mr. Summerbee and his wife are watching the sun sink below
the hills. The gulf between superficial social living and the
acting out of powerful instinctive forces is one of Powys's key
themes: perhaps the gulf between Thrushcross Grange and
Wuthering Heights.

*The Left Leg* is a striking achievement; fresh felicities come to
light with repeated readings. If Lawrence comes to mind it is
because of the gulf suggested above and because one of his
themes, like the main theme of *The Left Leg*, is self-destruction
and the link between self-destruction and destruction of others.
Nothing in *The Left Leg* approaches, it need hardly be said, the
profound inwardness with which the theme is treated and
realised in the persons of Gerald Crich, Gudrun, Loerke and

others. One might point to certain intrinsic weaknesses too. There does not seem to be sufficient reason for making James Gillet, the man who *did* say his prayers, so extremely unworldly: the ecstasy of prayer so takes hold of him that he can only be seen as altogether outside the scheme of this world's things: we never feel this sort of unreality about Mew, caricature though he is. Then there are moments when the touch is likely to seem more facetious than comic: the ruse by which Tom gets Susan Summerbee's garter, for instance, or the irruption of Mew's cows into the vicarage garden. On the other hand, most readers are likely to enjoy the comedy of Minnie Cuddy's suitors, bold in imagination and resourceful in making plans and timid when the opportunity comes along. The complex consciousness of T. F. Powys arising from a knowledge of intense feelings, from compassion and from a subtly delightful sense of humour, is already apparent in *The Left Leg*.

One says 'already' apparent. But the course of Powys's publication being what it was, it seems clear that *The Left Leg* was written later than some of the books which were subsequently published. It has the originalities of method which mark much of Powys, originalities sometimes appearing as no more than quirks of technique and sometimes carrying powerful effects.

This account of *The Left Leg* may have hinted at the way in which cross-references, verbal repetitions and echoes, recurrent images, form part of Powys's method. An instance from *Innocent Birds* will show with what deliberate art is revealed the 'gift' that God has promised to Madder village. In chapter XX, Mr. Tucker, preparing to open his book (the Bible) by the haystack, hears steps in the lane; it is Fred and Polly, the 'innocent' lovers, and when he realises they have stopped and are saying good-bye—Fred is going to Derby, 'in Spain', to make his fortune—Mr. Tucker presses his hands over his ears and buries his head in the straw stack. After some moments he comes out, and they are gone; with his hand in his pocket, touching his book,

He stood yet and listened, as though he expected
some sound to come to him.

It came, the deep continuous sound of distant waves
falling.

The force of the chapter is greatly increased when we recall a
previous incident. In chapter XIII, Mr. Solly, advised by *his*
talisman-book, goes to 'Boston', a half-built house, where he
will see who it is that is to receive God's gift. He overhears Fred
and Polly making love. He believes the gift is love, though,
strangely, he feels sad. He climbs Madder Hill, feeling more
and more gloomy as a dark mist envelops him:

Solly regarded mournfully the green summit of the
hill. It was that day as it had been yesterday, and as it
would be tomorrow. Solly listened. Distant sounds
have a peculiar value for the ear of a solitary man
upon a lonely hill. The trotting of a horse even can be
ominous. Solly now heard a sound as distant and as
fateful as that had been; he heard the waves of the sea.
Mrs. Crocker had never loved the sea; she used to say
that it was unkind and cruel, and once when two tiny
boys were drowned at Weyminster, she said sadly,
'Oh what a wicked monster the sea is!'

Mr. Solly heard the sea now . . .

The two lovers, the two listening men, the sounds of the sea:
then later, in chapter XXVI, Polly herself, lying in the copse
after her rape by Bugby, and with a confusion of memories and
thoughts in her mind, hears steps pass by—they sound like, and
are, Fred's—and then:

The evening was grown still, but with the ominous
stillness that tells of a storm that is coming. Polly heard
another sound that fell into stillness, but came again
more and more insistently. She listened, and the sound
grew louder, more weighted with heaviness, and more
clamorous in its call for the victim of the night.

Polly had heard the sea waves before when a storm
was either coming or else dying down in Madder.

Finally, the threatening of fate is ended for Fred and Polly when the waves, 'cruel by the eternal habit of a vast unconsciousness', take them in:

> The first wave they met drove them to shore again,
> but the return of it carried them out to meet another.
> This other wave was raised up above its fellows a
> great distance from the land. It was a proud wave,
> mountainous and black. It wasn't the kind of wave to
> run on in mere foam; it rolled heavy, it moved, a wall
> of dark waters. It was one of those huge waves that are
> only met with at night time on the high seas. It came
> out of the night and gathered the two drowning ones
> into its black womb. It broke upon them, and drew
> them by its undercurrent farther out to sea . .

Symbols and images recur in Powys to stress intentions, to emphasise actions and strengthen atmosphere. *Mark Only*, by his limitations almost cut off from everyday social living, is often seen with his horses on the skyline of the bleak hills; characteristically he fumbles with wires on a gatepost, or tries to mend harness by tying it up with string. In the same novel rats and ladders and ropes are associated with Tulk and his scheming. Old Peter Andrews meets his death on the rickety ladder. Tulk is hanged by the rope over his box-bed in the granary. Weasel and rabbit are introduced at several points in the narrative to make us think of James's pursuit of Nellie. The patter of dogs' feet, to Mark's mind symbolising death, is heard again and again. In fact the symbolism of *Mark Only* tends to be excessively visible in places, and though it is clearly the outcome of genuine and interesting technical enterprise— the real thing, and rare enough to be remarkable—and though it creates some very effective moments, we feel that it is some- times imposed from the outside rather than natural to the action and the dialogue. One of the effective moments is when Mark stands listening at the foot of the stairs on his wedding night; he thinks he hears something run by in the road—the dogs which never trouble him when he is in the stable, his real home and only refuge. He calls upstairs to Nellie, and hears the patter of her bare feet across the room: by that sound we feel that *she* is his fate. The range of the moment is further extended by her fearing that he really might have heard steps outside: these would be the steps of the prowling James, waiting for her.

In *Mockery Gap* the sea, bringer of life and beauty and fear and death, means many things, or rather one thing with many aspects. Mrs. Pring's notion of it, for instance, is stupid and comic but touched with human fearfulness and therefore in part pitiable; there is just a hint here of the pity that is to be such a strong ingredient in Powys's most considered and developed attitude to life:

> 'They jumping waters b'aint got all their senses,' Mrs. Pring had once informed Mr. Gulliver. And even poor unnoticed John Pottle, a character that the wise Wang might have written of, did notice as he carried Dinah's faggot—not out of politeness but only to hide himself the more—that the sea had departed, in a sulky fit of springtime madness, almost entirely out of sight.

And in the variable sea stands the Blind Cow Rock—it can be seen, and has this name, at Durdle Door, near Lulworth Cove— the eternal rock 'that alone of all natural objects had never been beguiled by the sunbeams into looking pretty.'

The point must arise of the solidity of the material upon which the technical methods can bite. To give a *full* sense of the inevitable approach of doom or of the variability of life (to take the instances just offered from *Innocent Birds* and *Mark Only* and *Mockery Gap*), it would be necessary to provide more substance in the men and women, particularly in the 'good' ones, than Powys normally provides. Even when we allow for his chosen way of presenting character 'in the flat', we have to admit that the single dimension of kindness or simple honesty or unworldly idealism of those who are opposed to the vicious, does not carry much weight. Mr. Solly in *Innocent Birds* is 'a kind one', but also 'a very babe in the world's doings'; and the idea conveyed by the very title of that novel suggests a restriction of the area of human behaviour that is being explored; tragic development is inhibited because the 'innocents' are lacking in experience and awareness. Similarly with Mark: both by his low mentality and his work on the lonely hill he seems to be outside the order of traditional sanctions:

> ' 'Tisn't Church weather', old Peter used to say,
> 'that do blow and frisky up on they stony mountains.'

Being thus apart from man, Mark is the special case, pathetic not tragic. The women whom we are to pity in *Mockery Gap* are vapid. In *Mr. Tasker's Gods* the people who are in opposition to the Rev. Hector Turnbull and other representatives of the unpleasant, do make a show of kindliness and clear-sightedness, but between them they are either too sadly resigned or implausibly idealistic. *Kindness in a Corner* is a comedy and so may be appraised by different standards in some things, but even here we feel an unwarrantable sadness of resignation in much of the presentation of the protagonist, the Rev. Silas Dottery. At best pathos, at worst sentimentality, is attached to the good characters in most of these stories.

Powys's intention to portray the element of 'everlasting mud' in man, is the source of the human monsters who inhabit the same world as the innocent and the simple good. Monsters, yet valid representatives of human traits. The writings of Shakespeare, Ben Jonson, Dickens, to name only three, abound with them. In *Mark Only* there is Charlie Tulk in his lust, his malice, his sadism, his complacency, his curiosity itch, his petty meannesses. We feel the peculiar horror of him as a calculating spectator of life, ceaselessly watching and plotting for things that will give him pleasure; he lives in cold moral insulation. Mr. Bugby in *Innocent Birds* is a sadist in small things and big, fly-crusher and wife-hurter. Miss Pettifer in the same novel and in others is the pseudo-religious snob lacking all charity. George Douse in *The Two Thieves* is like Tulk:

> His wishes were simple. He only wanted to see others
> suffer without suffering himself. He had a mind to get
> much and spend little.

C

A large number of Powysian characters of this kind could be cited.

There is no gloating or lusciousness in Powys's presentation of cruelty and callousness. Of callousness and cruelty, ranging from the quiet putting of obstacles in the way of an old woman's jam-making, to horse-beating and the stoning of cats, there is certainly a great deal, and if all his stories were like *The Two Thieves* there would be grounds for pronouncing him obsessed with the topic. But even in this disturbingly grim story where there is nothing that can be called amusing or humorous, control of the language is never lost:

> Grace crept into a corner of the room. She already felt the serpent growing in her womb. She tried to tear open her body with her nails: in three weeks she was measured for her coffin. The undertaker had expected her to be a little taller than she was. 'A beautiful corpse' he said smilingly.

(Grace's endeavour was to get rid of the child which George Douse had told her would be 'a hideous black serpent—the Devil's babe'.) The bare factual writing is far removed from indulgence. Moreover Douse is by various means 'placed' in a moral pattern which is powerfully implicit in the action. Cruelty in *The Two Thieves* looms large and is terrible; and it is condemned. (It may be noted here that *God*, *In Good Earth*, and *The Two Thieves* were published in 1932, and so do not properly come under the head of 'The Earlier Novels'.)

The unkindnesses, violences and brutalities of one of the better known novels, *Mr. Tasker's Gods*, are presented in such a way that far from being sado-masochistic they are seen to be ultimately an effect of distress and pity. The bitterness is tonic. It is hatred of cruelty and exploitation that makes *Mr. Tasker's Gods* such a savage exposure of the moral pretences of a society conditioned and ruled by money-values. One of the impressions that we take away from this novel is that at the time of its writing the author was under tremendous strain in contemplating man's inhumanity to man and to creatures. A passage from *Black Bryony* comes to mind here; it is where Mr. Morsay, the village clerk, walking across a field with Farmer Told and being regaled with a story of rat-poisoning, begins to be conscious of the pain in his side :

> He did not like the idea that it was possible for a human being to be in as great torment as a poisoned rat. The idea brought a man down.
>
> For by simply losing a book out of his own thatch, he might incur the risk of rolling round after his own heels in default of a proper tail.
>
> Mr. Morsay felt that after all a man was not so very far removed from the lower animals. He wished he was. The Clerk of Norbury rubbed his side.
>
> In front of him there was a large clod of earth. Mr. Morsay spitefully kicked the clod.
>
> The two men walked over the field together.
>
> They both watched a sea-gull that was lazily flying over their heads. The bird was splendidly large and white, its beautiful wings shone in the September sun.
>
> Mr. Told raised his gun to his shoulder and shot the sea-gull. The bird fluttered upon the ground in agony; it had been hit everywhere by the little, piercing, wounding shots.
>
> Mr. Morsay and Mr. Told watched the sea-gull flopping about and soiling its splendid wings with the clay sod.
>
> 'Another of them flying birds,' was Mr. Told's comment.
>
> The Clerk was pleased too, and began to feel better. It interested Mr. Morsay to see what a man made in God's own image could do when put to it.

The idiotic purpose, the obtuseness and the callousness are brought out starkly against the shining splendour of the 'lazily flying' bird.

Against the pain of knowledge Powys has what we may call the bulwark of creativity, of satisfaction in the thing made.

This is of course common to all genuine artists. More personal to Powys (though still, of course, common enough) are things like the frequent touches of social criticism: we have

>the member of Parliament for the Weyminster district,
>a gentleman who was once found at a social gathering
>shaking hands with the overcoats;

and there are the servile jurymen who

>could all write their own names except the thatcher,
>and he could set a drunken cross by the name of Sir
>Hugh Winterbottom at the elections.

There are passages where Swift comes to mind:

>With his beasts, Mr. Tasker was a perfect father: he
>waited by them at night when they were ill. Once he
>nearly killed his little girl—he hit her in the face with
>his hay-fork—because she had forgotten to carry a pail
>of water to a sick cow;

and from the same novel:

>He worked as a labourer upon one of the large farms,
>but his fancies led him to other tasks as well. He was
>the best man in the village at skinning a horse.

But incidental ironies of that sort are but precarious 'fragments shored against . . . ruins'. Is there anything more substantial that can serve as a pillar or a rock? Faith in the value of human love? It must be said that failure or death comes to nearly all the lovers in these novels. Polly and Fred (*Innocent Birds*) are easy victims of the vicious; Mr. Dottery (*Kindness in a Corner*) fails to seize the opportunity of a fuller life in love; the loves of the 'good' characters in *Mr. Tasker's Gods* are hopelessly idealistic and come to nothing anyway; John Gidden (*In Good Earth*) fails to find happiness in love. The fullest portrayal of love in these novels is in the story of Mr. Pattimore in *Mockery Gap*. It is worth giving in some detail.

The Rev. Pattimore was fifty-five when he married; his wife was twenty. Immediately after the honeymoon he began to take cold baths; under the influence of the Dean and St. Paul he 'now saw all young women, his young wife included, as wholesale temptations to wanton naughtiness.' For the next five years Mrs. Pattimore was starved of love. Her case, however, like that of the other unfulfilled women in the novel, is presented without force or sharpness. It is significant that she seems more concerned with baby clothes than with a relationship of love with her husband, but in spite of that pointer to the limited nature of her needs, Powys's portrayal of her remains on the whole sentimental. This is not so with Pattimore, whose stupidity in the continual stifling of his instincts for the sake of St. Paul and ecclesiastical preferment, is viewed sometimes with sardonic amusement and sometimes with an unsentimental compassion. Dinah Pottle is plump and attractive:

> Even Mr. Pattimore when Dinah passed him would be forced to clench his teeth and think of the Dean's gaiters in order to prevent himself from making a sound like a neigh.

But in the following passage, which comes when Mr. Pattimore, alone in the attic, is recalling his first and only love-making and thinking jealously at the same time of the pleasure his wife has shown in the company of the ape dressed in flowers (symbol of gay pleasure), it is not folly that is indicated. By a combination of sexual and nature imagery and verbal sound and compelling rhythm we are made to feel both his personal stress and the power of the forces demanding release:

> Mr. Pattimore sat up. He heard the midnight sea, the wicked one, the beautiful, the inspirer of a huge wickedness; he heard the sea. However much he had shut out from him all the gentle longings of his loving lady, this sound would come in. It came from the dark places of love, out of the bottom of the sea.
>
> It came naked, it stood before him as he had stood before her, as Milton's Adam new learned in love, in that pretty corner of the cliff where the blue butterflies were.
>
> He saw it as she must have seen him, through her fingers—all the male nakedness of the sea.

Dark movements were upon it, that came into him
with the sound. Dark movements, the purple blossoms
of the deep making their music.

The sound rose and fell, and Mr. Pattimore listened.

The ground swell splashed upon the Blind Cow
Rock.

Mr. Pattimore bit his finger to keep the noise away.

He turned over and slept.

Later, when through the agency of the fisherman he smashes
the Dean's picture and comes to Nellie, we are left in no doubt
about the rapacious quality of his love. She is delighted in the
reunion; but we wonder about their future. Love is of many
kinds in T. F. Powys.

The fisherman in *Mockery Gap*, like Mr. Weston and to a
certain extent John Death in *Unclay*, represents a warmth and
a generosity which are an opposing force to the malice of
circumstance that seems especially directed towards lovers.
Fair-bearded, he is most often seen in sunshine. He never
speaks. His expressions, particularly his smiling, speak for him.
Feared irrationally by several characters before he appears in
Mockery, and taunted by the children, when he comes, as the
ominous 'Nellie-bird', he shows himself gay, reckless, beautiful,
and wise. In his presence several people alter and are happier;
by his gift of love to a number of girls he helps to direct their
affairs to more successful ends. He is, of course, still feared by
some, and chivvied and insulted: he smiles at his traducers.
With his nets and his lavish gifts he is like Christ, but a Christ
who can be lightly wanton with his kindliness. He can be
serious and sad; there is an occasion when a number of
villagers, drawn by one another, have come down to the sea-
shore:

. . . The women moved nearer.

The holy peace of a summer's afternoon, sweet as
the scent of the lily-of-the-valley, visited the scene. The
green shade of the wood darkened the colour of the
sea, while the sea, with its tiny waves warmed, happily

danced. But the Blind Cow Rock cast a black shadow.

The women watched, holding out their hands. They expected at any moment to see the splash of the shining bodies of the fish.

They are disappointed. The fisherman is not singing. He sends the children and the youths away before he draws in his net, which holds two drowned women.

Corresponding to the part-human part-supernatural character in a Powys story are certain strangely charged moments and qualities of atmosphere, part-actual and part-remote. In *Mockery Gap* a sense of expectancy (impossible to suggest adequately in summary) pervades particularly the chapter entitled 'Miss Pink Fears Something is Coming'; the effects of the darkening sky on the gathering of life-fearing women at the vicarage sewing-party, of the thunder, of the (quite normal) entrance of the fisherman on the gravel drive, of the knocking, and finally the cloud breaking and the sun pouring down warmth as Mrs. Pattimore and the fisherman reappear, are rendered with the characteristic Powysian blending of solemnity and humour.

The final chapter—'A Perfect Gift'—of *Innocent Birds*, in atmosphere and method and tone foreshadows the effect of power and mystery, with the balance of a humane wisdom, which is so wonderfully achieved in many scenes of *Mr. Weston's Good Wine*. From the first sentence:

> Often the sea waves, although they christen them in
> the certainty of an everlasting reformation from all the
> old Adam, forget to name the dead that they give up.

—to the last, where Miss Pettifer throws Mr. Tucker's Bible on the fire, threads are being drawn together and correspondencies established simultaneously with the creation of atmosphere, of the feeling of time passing, of the mystery and actuality of Mr. Solly's visit by night to the churchyard; he has been drawn there by Mr. Tucker's lantern, and over the grave where the two drowned ones are buried they talk of the gift that has been given to Madder village:

'But the gift,' said Solly. 'What is the gift?' The
light in Susy's cottage went out. But the light in the
churchyard still shone.

The extinction of the cottage light means that Susy, the dowdy
and inefficient church-cleaner who prays in secret, has died;
and the lantern shines on the grave of Fred and Polly: the gift
of death has been given. The moment is enriched if at this
point we recall Mrs. Wimple's smacking little Polly for lying
about sun-kissed among the graves on the occasion of Mrs.
Pim's funeral; Mrs. Wimple feared that the parson would not
come into the churchyard while Polly was so unashamedly
revealing herself:

'How do 'ee think poor Annie can get put under dirt,
wi' 'ee a-showing all theeself to they nasty tombstones!'

Miss Pettifer may seem to have the last word in the novel, as
she throws Mr. Tucker's 'story-book' on the fire. But her
victory is hollow, we are made to feel that her action is
prompted by fear of what she has read on the last page:

And there shall be no light there; and they need no
candle, neither light of the sun; for the Lord God
giveth them light: and they shall reign for ever and
ever.

The collocation of churchyard and sun, the awareness of the
great symbolic force of each, are both effect and cause of
Powys's profound love of nature. Sun, sky, sea, grass, are
described for their sensuous beauty and for their power as
symbols. Sometimes the description emphasises a mood;
sometimes it points a development of attitude or of feeling.
When the severely self-disciplined Rev. Pattimore, for instance,
at the time of the beginning of his return to love, is walking
towards the sea, and the sun breaks through the clouds and
soaks Mockery in a bath of glory, his senses *will* be pleased
despite himself:

As Mr. Pattimore approached the waves, the same call
of beauty and all loveliness that had attracted his wife
earlier in the season now attracted him too. The

flowers had led her, the summer sounds led him. The sunlight danced and quivered upon the moving surface of the sea, the ripple of the tiny summer waves made happy music, while a three-masted barque, as if it knew the eyes of man wished it to be there, traversed the cool morning waters, with wide sails spread. A white sea-gull flew so low that it almost touched the ripples with its wings.

Mr. Pattimore walked upon the cool yellow sands.

He was conscious as he walked that the sands were shining. He looked quickly up at the blue sky, but found it shining too.

Then in *God*, a short novel whose fantasy-with-realism offers light-handedly something richer in naturalness and charitable feeling than the round of life that is conditioned by standard ideas of rectitude and success, the happy ending is in keeping with a general warmth, outward and inward:

No day could have been finer; the hot sun made the corn that was shocked in the fields crackle. There were so many blue butterflies upon the banks that they looked like violets in March. If one held out one's hand, the sun kissed it. No virgin need, that day, remain disconsolate; the holy Sun would lie with her.

It is near the close of that same story, *God*, that Mr. Vardy, the cobbler who reads Voltaire and laughs at most things but never at poverty or love, holds forth on man and nature:

Every autumn God dies, and in the spring He is given a new place in the lives of men, and is born again. It is the same with us; we die and go down to the pit, but until the worlds vanish, new life from our dust will arise and worship the sun.

This simple, confident note is not often sounded in Powys. What does emerge from the writings is an extraordinary attitude towards death, extraordinary in the depth of its acceptance. There is a section of *Kindness in a Corner* that illustrates it beautifully. Mr. and Mrs. Turtle, apart from a slight plot-connection with Canon Dibben's machinations, appear in the novel solely as a foil to the Rev. Dottery and sexton Truggin; they fear death:

> 'All true joys,' said Mr. Dottery, 'ought to lead us kindly to the grave, for they have given us a foretaste of heaven.'
>
> 'And that heaven be but a wormy sodden bed,' observed Mr. Turtle.
>
> 'No,' said Mr. Dottery, 'it is eternity.'
>
> 'And what be that?' asked Turtle.
>
> Mr. Dottery was silent.
>
> ' 'Tis what I do fear,' said Mrs. Turtle, with a shudder. 'For b'ain't we something now that do move and listen? In the early morning, doves do coo, and they loud village cocks do answer one another. Then the sounds of folk moving do begin, but soon we shall hear nothing, for, having lived, we shall live no more. . . .'
>
> 'Is there no way, then, to rid yourselves of your fear of death?' asked Mr. Dottery. 'Cannot you trust in God?'
>
> ' 'Tain't wise to put one's trust in a murderer,' replied Mr. Turtle.
>
> 'But cannot you think more kindly of death?' asked Mr. Dottery.
>
> Mr. Turtle shook his head.

The chapter entitled 'The Dirt of God' offers a superb instance of genius revivifying commonplaces with the unique personal touch. Truggin's speeches, their import and their rhythms, as he shows the Turtles the churchyard with the empty grave, come between small telling actions to produce a calm-bringing change and acquiescence in his hearers. A lover of his churchyard, Truggin is especially angered by the notion of a Day of Judgment:

> 'Is God a thief?' he said to the Turtles. 'Is he a stealing Welshman that He should call up folk's

bones from where they be laid? Where is the sense or
reason in changing a man's clothes, who be well
content with a suit of earth, soft as any flannel
drawers? Who would wish to throw into a huge
disorder the holy silence, and where be any content
to equal the happiness of this pretty garden? All who
lie here do wish to stay for ever. Don't 'ee listen to
none of thik foolish risen talk, don't 'ee never learn to
look up. 'Tis best to look down for comfort, for when
a perfect state be reached, what more need be said or
done?'

As 'the soft gloom of the warm, still night, together with a
sweet, earthy scent, entered into the Turtles, so that they
gently wept', Truggin takes up a little soil:

' 'Tain't earth that I do hold,' he said, ' 'tisn't earth
at all, here be the dirt of God. There b'ain't no stone,
no root of grass, no mould, that be man's here—'tis
God's. Our lively doings in the world are ours, here
our rottenness be God's.'

In these speeches the unpleasant connotations of 'dirt' and
'rottenness' disappear; a transformation of customary modes of
thinking and feeling takes place. The gruesome and the fearful
have been assimilated in a calm vision:

'No man,' he observed, 'need fear to die alone.
During a little time, that be but a moment to him, all
they that have known him in his lifetime be laid down
too. Or ever the cool earth do mingle wi' 'is bones, two
generations will be gone. And above them all, the
grass do show as green as when they lived. Bones do
work upwards—soon a poor man do get near to the
world again. And what be this earthy covering? 'Tis
only a fine lasting blanket that be tucked close, above
which they little birds do twit and peck.

'Footfalls do pass, new folk do walk above, small
rains fall soft, and the snowdrops do show. Winnie
Croot do skip over Tadnol bridge. She be a little girl

to have such quick legs, but she don't go no faster
across river than a man do move from his coming to
his going in his earthly pilgrimage . . . As a ploughman do stretch 'is eye over a furrow that hath no
end, so a man do look who be dying.

'Life is a little matter, 'tis but a moment in a
hollow tree wi' a naughty maid, 'tis now come, 'tis
now gone.'

'Thik be a wide and vast place', said Truggin,
climbing out of the grave and pointing back to it,
'though it do look so small. God, who do but lend
'Is love to the living, do give it to the dead for all
time. There b'ain't no clod that do touch a bone that
does not love with a greater love than the living do
know of. And what be loneliness but to bide in our
sorrows, for time b'ain't always kind?'

There is no last word on death. But Truggin is extremely
persuasive. Bleakness is dissolved in his homeliness and
assurance. It is typical of Powys to follow 'The Dirt of God'
with a chapter which describes the farcical antics of Canon
Dibben as he essays to put in motion his plan for the purification
of Mr. Dottery's soul.

Ultimately we shall be likely to see most of these works
mainly in the aspect of lesser writings by the author of *Mr.
Weston's Good Wine* and *Fables*.   But when we have put aside
the dreary insistence on gloom, the overplayed crotchets and
idiosyncrasies of certain characters, the lurid portentousness,
the narrative-irrelevancies, the flat literalness alternating with
melodramatic over-emphasis, which make *Hester Dominy* and
*Abraham Men* and *Black Bryony* (despite interesting bits) the
poorest of these novels, and which mar some of the others, we
can see enough of interesting technical method applied to the
expression of an extremely interesting vision of life, to make
us feel Powys's potentiality. In *The Left Leg*, *God*, *In Good
Earth*, *The Two Thieves*, and in many parts of the others, the
material is organized in such a way and presented (often) in

a prose of such distinction that no discriminating reader would fail to make the inward comment that he is here in touch with a profoundly original literary artist. Such a reader would not be surprised, coming for the first time upon it, by the perfection of the deliberate, formal art, formal without loss of feeling, of *Mr. Weston's Good Wine* and *Fables*.

*Chapter Three*

## MR. WESTON'S GOOD WINE

AND WE—we will have no garish sunshine in our story,
but only a long evening to prepare us for the everlasting night.

The words occur when Thomas Bunce, setting a match to the
parlour fire, ushers in that immortal evening at the Angel Inn.
Reinforced by certain words spoken by Mr. Weston to Luke
Bird, they might well, if taken by themselves, predispose a
reader to an idea of the story as one of determined gloom.
Referring to himself as a writer—of the Bible, of course—Mr.
Weston says:

' . . . I put as much, nay rather more, hope into my
book, to its hurt I fear, than anyone else. You must
know that pessimism is the best and most enduring
wear from cover to cover.'

And yet *Mr. Weston's Good Wine*, though tragic in its
recognitions of evil, of men's blindness, weakness, and failures,
of their common fate in death, is tragic also in the profound
sympathy, the more profound because it is always intelligent
and unsentimental, with which Powys observes and comments
on the human scene; it gives support to Yeats's utterance:
'We begin to live when we have conceived life as tragedy'.

46

*Mr. Weston's Good Wine*, considered as a vision of human life, is certainly not more pessimistic, in the customary sense of the word, than *The Tempest*. The general lightness of touch, the humour, the breadth of Mr. Weston's humanity, are played off against the 'dark' elements with something of the effect that Shakespeare's poetry and Prospero's authority have in contrast and combination with the motives and actions of Caliban, Sebastian and company.

It is Powys's masterpiece because it is his fullest and most perfect artistic utterance. It is without the faults that mar many of the longer works: exaggerated intensities and violences, Dickensian repetitiousness in the matter of idiosyncrasies and fancies, lack of satisfying positive values as embodied in people (as distinct from enrichening pleasure in nature and contemplation), the flatness of an unforceful realism, whims of structure both in chapter- and paragraph-sequence. One or more of these is likely to be found, in these works, jostling the corresponding things of force, delicacy, and beauty. This is not so in *Mr. Weston*, where the communication of a mastery over a wide range of experience is achieved with scarcely a jarring note.

It has been my experience to hear more than one reader speak warmly and admiringly of *Mr. Weston's Good Wine*, while at the same time being uneasy about its 'meaning'. Everything that happens is clearly enough understood, but the character and function of Mr. Weston, and with him Michael, do not for many readers fit into either allegory or realism. It is somehow felt to be disconcerting to receive the impact of so much actual village life at the same time as having to keep in mind throughout that Mr. Weston is 'God'. And yet, do we have to keep it in mind? Once realised, is not the allegorical significance taken up, with an easy perfection, into the whole work? There ought to be no more difficulty in accepting the *Good Wine* than there is in accepting *The Tempest*. The power and nature of its language should be its warranty.

Acceptance of the mode doesn't of course guarantee

immediate understanding of the whole novel. There are cruxes in the *Good Wine* which require a good deal of pondering. But despite their presence, and however puzzling they may be, the novel as a whole is no more 'strange' than (say) *The Scarlet Letter* or *What Maisie Knew*.

*Mr. Weston's Good Wine* opens with a plain statement:

> A Ford car, of a type that is commonly used in England to deliver goods in rural districts, stood, at half-past three in the afternoon, before the Rod and Lion Hotel at Maidenbridge upon the 20th November, 1923.

The facts given about the car (it was a covered one, it was by no means new, and it was muddy), about the driver and the lurking children and the passing lady, together with the evocation—by narrative and not description—of the autumnal lethargy of the little town, convey a strong sense of actuality. The lethargy is of course quite delusive. The novelist sees and senses the life in the apparent lack of liveliness. A passage in *Emma* has both details and a general tenor which are like things in this first chapter of *Mr. Weston:*

> Much could not be hoped from the traffic of even the busiest part of Highbury; Mr. Perry walking hastily by, Mr. William Cox letting himself in at the office door, Mr. Cole's carriage horses returning from exercise, or a stray letter-boy on an obstinate mule, were the liveliest objects she could presume to expect; and when her eyes fell only on the butcher with his tray, a tidy old woman travelling homewards from shop with her full basket, two curs quarrelling over a dirty bone, and a string of dawdling children round the baker's little bow-window eyeing the gingerbread, she knew she had no reason to complain, and was amused enough; quite enough still to stand at the door. A mind lively and at ease, can do with seeing nothing, and can see nothing that does not answer.

But as always Powys transforms 'influence' into something

original and creative, and the simple-seeming chapter ends with a lad's 'fear and horror' and his flight from what he saw when he opened the curtain and peeped in at the back of the car. (His flight, we are later told, had not passed unnoticed by Mr. Weston, who shook his head a little sternly but smiled too.) There are dangerous forces beneath the surface of the placid everyday world. Likewise, in the second chapter, the world of the simple and loving Miss Gipps is transformed by the curiously pleasant effect wrought on her by the sight of Mr. Weston and of Michael, and by reading the words on the car, especially the lovely word, 'wine'. At the end of the chapter,

> Miss Gipps saw a new vision of life, happy and joyous, all love and no shame, with malice and meanness and envy departed for ever.

And she saw herself the happy wife of Mr. Board. Between the horror of 'whatever it was that Tom had seen', and the joy-bringing illusion of the inexperienced Miss Gipps, is played out the varied drama of human feelings, thoughts, attitudes, behaviour, and habits, which constitute the substance of *Mr. Weston's Good Wine*. The substance is bound together and given significance and beauty by the superbly maintained tone and by the function and pervasive presence of Mr. Weston. To discuss Mr. Weston in any fullness will be to discuss tone also: his wisdom, with its goodness and humour, resides in his tone and manner as firmly as it appears in his actions.

Mr. Weston, then, comes to the village of Folly Down, on a dull November evening, in a Ford car. For many readers of the mid-twentieth century the old 'T' model Ford represented in its day, efficiency; an efficiency inexpensive and unpretentious. It was regarded, mainly because it bumped and rattled along, with a certain kindly amusement, but its sterling performance was a matter of common talk. (George Charlton's drawing in the 1927 *Mr. Weston's Good Wine* shows well what it looked like.) Without suggesting that the *Good Wine* leans with anything but the lightest weight on the character and appearance of that Ford in 1923, it is of course wholly Powysian that the car should

D

have been what it was and not a Daimler or a Rolls Royce.
Mr. Weston, it is true, is a tradesman but he is also God, come
to earth in His chariot to observe, for an evening which is also
an eternity, the affairs of mankind and to comment, to intervene,
to judge, to punish, to pity, to  guide. This account of Mr.
Weston, with its suggestion of a Prospero-like function, is of
course an abstract from the novel. Powys never explains in the
way a critic or a reader sometimes has to explain. We are *shown*
Mr. Weston with all his movements, speeches, gestures,
expressions. What he stands for, what he teaches, come out of
our delighted recognition of what he *is*.

Mr. Weston dispenses two wines, one light and one dark,
the light wine of love, and the dark wine of death: love and
death, called elsewhere by Powys the 'two great realities'. Both
wines are 'good wine'; in fact, they are really the same wine,
but of different strengths; and Mr. Weston trades in both. He
is a wise tradesman, he studies the habits, the manners, the
wants of his customers:

> Evidently, before Mr. Weston set out upon his travels
> he had made careful and detailed enquiries, so that he
> might know beforehand the kind of people that he was
> to meet and most probably trade with.

It is easy to see that Powys is able, with such a conception, to
exhibit as it were a reflection of his own wisdom in the character
of a man, or 'God', who has keenly observed and deeply
considered the ways of human beings in love and in death.
Sorrow, pity, delight mingle in the contemplation of human life.
Sorrow is not dwelt on overmuch, delight does not preclude a
sympathetic outgoing of feeling.

Mr. Weston is both the naïve happy *viveur* and the punitive
judge. The man who rubs his hands gleefully when Michael
reads out the name of the landlord of the Angel Inn is also the
man who has the grave of Ada Kiddle opened so that her
decaying body may be seen by her seducers. He is responsive
to everyone and to every situation; but he is never incapacitated
by emotion. He acts when action is timely, he passes judgment

when the occasion demands it. He listens with complete sympathetic seriousness to Michael's somewhat heightened account of the Rev. Grobe's sorrow, but he sees it in proportion and knows how to deal with it:

'. . . Upon such an evening, when the right silence reigns, Mr. Grobe's melancholy feeds upon itself; his sorrow lingers and hovers in the dark corners of the room that are away from the light. . . The glorious summer, the hot noon of all the seasons, only dooms his steps to falter; and the harvest saddens him, for that season shows how all things, even a green blade of corn, tend to their end. It is only a long autumn evening that can soothe Mr. Grobe's soul.'

'The very man for our good wine,' said Mr. Weston cheerfully.

It is in part the readiness of his responses, the emotional quickness, that make Mr. Weston so much more complete, both as a human and an allegorical figure, than Squire Jar ever is, or John Death in *Unclay*. A host of adverbs and phrases are used to suggest the variety: 'easy and friendly manner', 'guiding the car carefully round a corner', 'thoughtfully', 'laid his hand affectionately upon his companion's knee', 'excitedly', 'gleefully', 'smiling' (this frequently occurs), 'slapping his knee', 'eagerly', 'chuckled', 'tenderly', 'with a slight frown', 'happy and easy at the inn', 'nodded in a good-humoured manner', 'sternly', 'placing his hand upon the landlord's shoulder and gently compelling him to sit down again', 'bowing politely to the landlord', 'gratefully', 'blushed', 'rubbing his hands joyfully', 'in deep disappointment'. Mr. Weston is widely and sharply subject to human feelings. He is not infallible; Michael occasionally seems more right than his master. By hints here and there of Mr. Weston's lack of absolute wisdom Powys keeps him human and thereby makes his judgment and his authority the more compelling.

An assemblage of adverbs and phrases has its use, but it is only in continuous sequences that Mr. Weston can be seen

moving with human interest and with understanding and
power among the familiarities of everyday life. Interest,
understanding, and power: they are qualities of the writing
too, qualities of Powys himself.

Human sympathy, memories of beauty and joy, disenchantment, are unified in the scene where Mr. Weston stands on the
hill as evening approaches, and after contemplation holds out
his hands in blessing over the village:

> Standing upon the barren hill, Mr. Weston wished
> to see Folly Down as it was in the summer. He had
> only to wish, and the fancy with which he was gifted
> would complete the matter.
>
> Mr. Weston now saw Folly Down in its gayer days:
> he created the summer anew as he looked down the
> valley. The hedges were white with sloe blossom, and
> the willow bushes were in flower; a few butterflies
> were abroad and the bumble bees. The blackthorn
> blossoms were shed; the new green of the hedges came,
> and the sweet scent of may blossom. The may faded,
> but in the meadows the deeper colour of the butter-
> cups—those June brides—took the place of the
> maiden cowslips until the hay-mowers came, and
> then the white and red roses bloomed in the hedges.
> Midsummer, that time of rich sunshine, was soon
> gone; the meadows were yellow again with hawkweed,
> while in the rougher fields the ragwort grew in
> clumps, upon which the peacock butterflies fed until
> near drunken with honey.
>
> Mr. Weston let the summer go. The scented seasons
> he had seen in his fancy fled away again and were
> gone.
>
> Mr. Weston felt lonely. The same mood that he
> remembered having when he was writing his book
> came to him again. He climbed a tumulus in the
> gathering darkness, and regarded all the earth with
> a lonely pity.

A wind awoke from the sea that was but a mile or two away, and rushed and roared about him. Mr. Weston took off his hat, and the wind blew his white hair. He was evidently glad, as any city dweller would be, to be standing there.

'There are some people,' said Mr. Weston aloud, 'who, I believe, envy my position in the city where I live, but they are wrong to do so, for I would willingly exchange all that I am with any simple child that lives and dies in these gentle valleys, and is then forgotten.'

Mr. Weston stretched out his hands over the village of Folly Down. He came down from the mound and returned to the car.

A similar balance of sympathy and solemnity, solemnity without inflation, is felt when Mr. Weston reminds Michael of the richly varied interests of his book, and of the properties of his dark wine:

'. . . The rich and prosperous, alas! are so often filled with so many expensive wines that, when they come to ours, they pretend that it tastes a little sour. You know my poetry, Michael?' Michael blushed.

Mr. Weston smiled. 'Do not be alarmed. I am no Wordsworth—I will not recite to you now, and besides, I can never remember my best songs. I was but going to mention that, in my book, I have noted and taken into account all the vagaries of human nature from its first beginning, so that my book is really intended to assist us to trade. All the way through my book—but you know it, Michael'— (Michael blushed again)—'I speak of a wine, some of which we carry with us now, that, though we do not advertise it as medicinal, yet, as you very well know, there is no trouble incident to the fretful and changing life of man that this particular wine will not cure for ever.

'We have had customers,' continued Mr. Weston, speaking in a lower tone, 'who have sometimes invited themselves—and I, even I have always attended them there—into our deepest and most dingy cellar, upon the walls of which are green mould and cobwebs, and upon the floors toads and vipers. To taste this wine of ours that has never seen daylight is the desire of some of the most noble of our customers.'

'And those,' said Michael, 'who go down with you to taste that wine have no booked orders for what they buy. They pay ready cash, and owe us no more.'

'Yes,' said Mr. Weston, 'we allow no credit for that wine.'

The allegorical mode allows the horror and finality of death to be starkly enough presented, but at the same time carries humour, humanity, and unstrained control. Later, the same note is to be struck when in a beautifully developed dialogue Mr. Grobe is taught the virtues of the 'dark wine of a high price':

Mr. Weston was by no means the sort of trader to keep anyone in suspense as to what he had to sell.

'I am a wine merchant,' he said, as soon as he was seated. 'I am able to supply a very good wine at a low price. I give ten per cent discount for ready money. My wine is new.'

'But I am afraid,' replied Mr. Grobe, 'that I prefer old wine.'

'My firm,' said Mr. Weston, 'has been established a long time, and when I describe the wine that I am offering you as new, I do so but to contrast this vintage with our oldest and strongest wine, many pipes of which we always store in bond, but only deliver when a very special request is made.'

'A dark wine of a high price, I suppose?' said Mr. Grobe.

'Yes, a deadly wine,' replied Mr. Weston in a low

voice. 'And by no means to the taste of Landlord Bunce,' he added, smiling.

'No, no,' said Mr. Weston, looking curiously at Mr. Grobe, 'the wine that I like best to offer to the public—for, though I hate nothing that I have made, I prefer to sell this lighter kind—compared to our oldest is very new, and this wine can be drunk at all times without the chance of a headache.'

'Do not, I pray you, think my question a strange one, Mr. Weston,' said Mr. Grobe, 'but do you yourself ever drink that deadly wine that you speak of?'

'The day will come when I hope to drink of it', replied Mr. Weston gravely, 'but when I drink my own deadly wine the firm will end.'

'And your customers?' asked Mr. Grobe.

'Will all drink of it too,' said Mr. Weston.

'Ah,' observed Mr. Grobe, 'it would be better, I think, to begin with your milder wine.'

'Mr. Grobe be right enough there,' laughed Mr. Bunce, 'for most like, thik dark wine Mr. Weston do name would make a man so dead drunk that 'e wouldn't know nothing no more.'

'You never spoke a truer word in your life, landlord,' said Mr. Weston.

As the action proceeds, Mr. Weston shows himself more and more to be the judge with power and mercy. When he encounters Grunter in the church, the only church he has ever entered—he prefers inns—and after some talk of the ways of love and sin, gives him the order to open Ada's grave, the writing evokes superbly a sense of the momentous: with echoes of the New Testament and Christ perfectly fused with the familiarities of a normal human interchange, it is charged with a religious feeling that is neither over-exalted nor self-righteous:

Mr. Grunter edged himself away. Ever since Mr. Weston had called himself a writer, he had regarded him with suspicion, and he now wished himself out of his company.

'A poor man,' he grumbled 'mid have to get 'is own living in Eternity as well as in time, and even if this evening do last for ever, me wold 'oman will mind when supper time do come.'

Mr. Grunter stepped back, but the wine-merchant touched his arm.

'I have work for you to do, John Grunter,' he said.

'And who be thee to command folk?' asked the clerk.

Mr. Weston uncovered his head and looked at him. Until that moment he had kept on his hat.

'Who be thee?' asked Grunter in a lower tone . . .

'I know thee now,' said Mr. Grunter.

'Then tell no man,' said Mr. Weston.

Mr. Grunter looked happy; he even grinned.

'I did fancy at first,' he said in a familiar tone, 'that thee was the devil, and so I did walk down church aisle behind 'ee to see if thee's tail did show.'

Mr. Weston told the clerk what he wished him to do. Grunter started back in fright.

'But she drank of my best wine,' said Mr. Weston.

'Don't 'ee waste none of thik wine upon I,' cried Mr. Grunter, shrinking away, 'for thik wine be too strong for a poor man who bain't used to drinking.'

Mr. Weston smiled. The clerk looked at him gloomily.

'All they t'other dead bain't got to rise to-night?' he enquired, 'for wold grandfather did promise to beat I wi' 'is Sunday walking-stick if ever he got me hold in heaven, and what if Potten who be buried under elm tree do begin to talk?'

'No,' said Mr. Weston, 'you must only open one grave to-night, Grunter.'

Grunter, the church-clerk who in common repute is wrongly held to be the great seducer of Folly Down, duly opens the grave, the grave in which he had unknowingly buried a boot when he had previously filled it in. It is in the chapter entitled 'Mr. Grunter Finds his Lost Boot' that the punishment of the Mumby brothers, who are the real seducers and the virtual murderers of Ada, begins. It is a magnificent chapter, combining compassion with the moral force of a medieval or Elizabethan *memento mori*, assimilating the intense, the delicate, the comic, and making a harmony of them. In the first half of the chapter, atmospheric touches and brief factual sentences suggest the growing terrors of the young men, who have been told that a bottle of wine is waiting for them in the churchyard. Then we come to this:

> Mr. Weston hurried them on. They followed the path and came to the other side of the yew tree, where they nearly walked into a heap of earth, an open coffin, and Mr. Grunter.
>
> The Mumbys, too stricken with terror to know what to do, looked at Mr. Grunter, who was carefully examining an old boot that he held in his hand.
>
> Mr. Grunter looked at the boot very carefully by the light of his lantern. He was deciding whether anything could be done towards mending it by the local cobbler.
>
> There is a strange power that often compels a man to look upon what he most wishes to avoid. This same power forced the Mumbys to see what was there.
>
> What was there was Ada, but not the Ada whom they had known, but only the body corrupted, the soiled thing, the weeping clod.
>
> Mr. Grunter smiled at his boot; he believed that something might be done to it. He laid the boot carefully down and looked at Ada.
>
> The coffin he had easily unearthed, for it was not his custom to bury anyone deeper than must be, and the coffin lid, as he had expected, was all but rotted through.

'My good wine, gentlemen,' said Mr. Weston.

Though the worms had destroyed Ada's beauty, her shape was still there, and Mr. Grunter regarded her compassionately. He saw Ada as if she were a picture, which is the way that all wise countrymen regard the world or anything in it that seems a little curious or out of the common.

'When life bain't,' said Mr. Grunter slowly, 'death be.'

Mr. Grunter recalled to his mind that Ada Kiddle had once been a pretty living thing of blonde flesh, and he looked thoughtfully at her.

A picture may move a man, and this picture affected Mr. Grunter.

Mr. Grunter stood back a pace or two and then addressed the company.

'I bain't going to be famous no more,' he said. 'I don't want no woon no more to mention I. I don't want to be noticed. I would rather bide about and be nothing.

'Ada,' he said, stepping to the coffin again, ' tain't I that have moulded 'ee, 'tain't I that have rotted thee's merry ways wi' wormy clay. I bain't to be talked of no more.'

Martin Mumby was less cowed now. Mr. Grunter's remarks had made him feel more like himself again, and Martin noticed, too, that Mr. Weston had covered his face with his hands, as if he wept.

'You are a liar and a cheat,' Martin shouted at the wine merchant. 'You promised us wine, and you show us the rotted corpse of a whore. Is this your wine?'

Mr. Weston said nothing.

Mr. Weston's silence is the silence of Christ before his accusers. It seems also to be, in small part, acquiescence; for he has more than once shown his sorrow for the burden and the doom that he has assigned to men, and more than once expressed his longing for the day when he will drink his own dark wine.

Michael is an admirable conception as companion and foil to Mr. Weston. Mr. Weston is rather short and plump; his brown felt hat covers hair that is 'white like wool'; his grey eyes are thoughtful, despite the twinkle of merriment that frequently lights them up; his face is 'good-natured and loving, though a trifle rugged and worn'. Michael is a tall young man, almost god-like in his beauty and manner as his toes scarcely touch the ground he treads upon. But this being who, we are made to feel, is himself worthy of worship,

> behaved to Mr. Weston with a respect that did honour to them both, for it was the loving respect that is never given unless the object is entirely deserving of it. This respect was utterly natural and unassumed, and was by no means dictated by the immense magnitude and long standing of the firm of which Mr. Weston was the senior director, but came rather from the love of one good heart to another—a more lofty and an older one.

It is Michael who provides Mr. Weston (and the reader) with the information he needs about Folly Down and its inhabitants. His liveliness, and the quickness of his reactions, and the nature of his comments, add to the fullness of the vision that we are being given. There are moments when his alert capacity for sensual appreciativeness, his frankness and freedom of outlook and speech, strike across a certain 'old-fashionedness' in Mr. Weston, producing an enhancing and liberating breadth-with-keenness. In particular, love deeply interests him. Mr. Weston, reading through the names of the villagers in his book, comes to Tamar Grobe, and asks Michael to tell him about her:

> 'With the greatest willingness,' answered Michael, 'for I know her very well. She has a brown birth-mark about the size of a sixpence, just a little above her navel.'

'You particularise too much, Michael.'

'She is dark; she has red, pouting lips; she is neither short nor tall. She has a cherub face and pleasant breasts, well suited to such a maiden. Her ankles are very small, and her gait free though yielding; and she refuses to leave her father for anyone lower than an angel. Would you care to hear any more about her?'

'As much as you may think proper to tell me,' said Mr. Weston eagerly.

'Tamar is indeed a lovely creature,' continued Michael fervently.

He suggests that this 'longing girl', who never pretends to be anything but what she is, 'looks too high' for a lover; she expects too much of love. Later he is equally frank about Jenny Bunce's plump beauty, and sensuously indicates her seductiveness,

'But even though her eyes are so merry, Jenny Bunce is no wanton, and her whole idea of happiness in this life, and in the life to come, is to have a cottage of her own and to be married to a good man.'

At the time of the story it is Jenny whom Mrs. Vosper wants to see in trouble, for Mrs. Vosper is ageing and jealous, and therefore cruel. She 'has a mind to see a girl forced,' says Michael, whose speech is notably forthright. He continues:

'She has much on her side, for country men have often grosser manners and less feeling than any orang-outang in an African forest . . . '

Previously he has drily announced that

'Mrs. Vosper's Christian name is Jane, and her interest in life is concupiscence.'

Clearly Michael, while being used as an expression of experience in the ways of love and lust, has also on occasions the function of a judge. But mainly he is warm-hearted and delightful.

His account of the betrayal of Ada Kiddle by Martin Mumby

suggests the ambiguities and conflicting elements inherent in love, lust, beauty, in life itself. Perfection of natural beauty may go with lust and with death:

'The fair midsummer day turned to evening; the swallows had fed their second batch of hungry, open mouths, and were tired of flying in and out of Mr. Mumby's cart-shed; the evening gnats hung in the air as if painted upon it, and Mrs. Vosper and Ada Kiddle stood with a young man under the oak tree.

'They stood near to one another, there in the slow-dying and coloured light of a summer's evening. At this time and season, more than any other, a vision of living beauty, a fair being of delight moves in the twilight. This presence can only be known and loved —for it casts a deep peace around it—by those minds'—('inspired by our wine,' suggested Mr. Weston)—'that are freed from all gross and carnal thoughts and imaginings, and that can merge and deliver themselves into the hands of eternal beauty. Upon such an evening even the Creator of the universe can wish to forget Himself for a season and be born again, in the exquisite loveliness of one lonely daisy.'

'And would that He might so forget Himself!' said Mr. Weston sadly.

When the winter gales had shaken off the last leaves from the oak tree, Michael continues, Ada, now with child, forwarded her request for a bottle of the blackest and strongest wine. While Mr. Weston himself, telling Michael he has never been inside a church—'Michael looked a little surprised'—gives further disturbing but broadening hints of complexities when he says with a certain grim and witty conciseness:

'I only like to go . . . where my good wine is drunk. In a condemned cell, in a brothel, in the kennels of a vast city, our wine is drunk to the dregs, but in a church they merely sip.'

When specific passages occur that are plainly 'allegorical' by virtue of their reference to Bible matters, the tone has the same easy breadth which characterises Mr. Weston and Michael themselves and which pervades the whole narrative. When Michael makes his first appearance it is as 'a partner in Mr. Weston's concern'; the glorious Archangel's fight against Satan in Heaven is in these terms:

> This gentleman had risen to high distinction in the firm, having once, by his strength and courage, quelled a mutiny that arose amongst the workers in Mr. Weston's bottling department—a mutiny that, had it been successful, would have entirely ruined the wine merchant's vast business, whose ramifications were everywhere.

The familiarities of trade-talk take in, without strain, Biblical language and solemn considerations; the sparrow that does not fall unseen is given a Powysian touch, the fate of 'the only son of the founder' is lightly but none the less certainly indicated:

> But a firm that is pretty well established in the world and has a very large surplus of capital, may be allowed its whim, which in this case was, we may almost say, to take note of a sparrow that, in flying after its mate a little too hastily from a bough to the thatch, chances to fall. And, indeed, any expert in business must acquiesce here, and agree that, though the actual gain in money may be small, it certainly pays the management of a large store to send a representative—though, perhaps, not the only son of the founder—into the less populated villages, where he may study at first hand the needs of simple people in order to ease them of their pennies.

Christ's hard lot is again recalled when Michael, telling about Luke Bird who lives 'in a very poor way' and who feeds the robins with crumbs, quotes to his master, with the right apologetic note, from Isaiah: 'He is despised, and I will add, if you have no objection, he is rejected of men.' And indeed the thought of 'men's' behaviour, of man's planting in the Garden of Eden, and of his subsequent history, does often sadden Mr. Weston and occasionally embitter him: he

> couldn't help recollecting then how, in a childish fit of mischief, he had once planted a long snaky root in his mother's flower plot that grew in the summertime into a horrid patch of nettles that deserved only to be utterly burnt and destroyed.

(In the *Penguin* edition 'snaky' is unfortunately printed as 'shaky'.)

One of the effects of the inclusiveness of Powys's imaginative sympathies is to give to his writing the kind of force and interest which is found often in, say, Langland and Bunyan, and sometimes in Swift. The harmonising of heterogeneous elements in story and in style springs out of a spirit that is fine because it is truly democratic. The oak-tree bed itself, symbolising the multiple manifestations of love, is the scene of sharply varied episodes: it is there that Jenny Bunce is saved from her would-be ravishers by Mr. Grunter's astonished shout at seeing Mr. Weston's advertisement in the sky; Mr. Grunter, preparing to hang himself from the tree, is himself saved by the laughing kindness of Alice Grobe, she who 'has with her all the wild, naughty ways of a spoilt child that knew nothing, only love'; Ada Kiddle's suicide comes from 'love' on the mossy bed; Tamar, eager for an intense pure love, 'would lie down in the bed; she would press her lips against the tree, with an ardour that showed well with what an agony of passion she would receive her lover when he at last came to her', and she is finally embraced there by Michael; it is in the tree that the faithful, gentle and generously loving Luke Bird finds his future lover and wife, Jenny. The variety of incident is unified by Powys's catholic spirit and artistic purpose. In the same way, transcendentalisms rest easily but significantly side by side with day-to-dayness. Tamar's unearthly love takes her into the skies on the same page that Mrs. Bunce insists that she

b'ain't satisfied about the quantity of the onions she has pickled.
Solemn, deep words—

> I form the light, and create darkness: I make peace,
> and create evil; I, the Lord, do all these things—

are heard as Mr. Weston, provoked and amused by the Angel
Inn conversation about God's doings, 'hid his face in his mug
and took a very deep draught'. Character and moral issues are
(in some cases) adumbrated with the cool sharp tone of
experience; as when Michael is describing Mr. Mumby, the
Folly Down squire:

> ' . . . and he owns the land and a meek wife. He
> possesses three elderly and plain maidservants, blames
> the weather a great many times in the day, and has
> two sons who prefer fornication to married bliss.'

The juxtapositions, the kind of wit involved, are not
autonomous clevernesses but are inseparable from the progress
and totality of the story. Moreover there are many passages of
an easy-flowing eloquence, which, while it is controlled towards
the significant issues and ends in view, is eager and warm.
Quotation would have to be inconveniently lengthy to support
these points, but I do not think they are likely to be disputed
by anyone who recalls or turns up the pages where (say)
Michael explains the difference wrought on the earth and on
people by the coming of darkness, or where he describes the
sorrowing state of Mr. Grobe, or where Mr. Weston stands on
the hill and surveys Folly Down, or where the spirit of the
Angel Inn (at the end of chapter XVII) is conveyed.

There is no need here to demonstrate in any fullness the
effectiveness of the specifically dramatic moments in the novel,
of the evocations of atmosphere, of the humour of the rustic
dialogue as distinct from the profounder colloquies. These
things are there for all to see. The numerous realistic descriptions and the gestures and speech of every day mingle with
scenes like that in which chilly horror descends on Mrs. Vosper's
'love'-parlour, when the 'clammy damp wound in coils about
the girls', with the momentous silence and the stopping of time

in the Angel Inn parlour, with the exultant encounter in love
of Tamar and Michael, with strange steps heard, with the
moments when the words 'Mr. Weston's Good Wine' are
spoken, and so on: they add up to a total 'atmosphere' where
actuality and the temporal are firmly grasped and at the same
time given a visionary quality embracing both physical and
moral significances.

Nor is it necessary at this juncture to do more than touch
upon the presence of topics and themes which enrich and
diversify the whole. For instance, there is the question of
responsibility, of man's free will: is it God or Mr. Grunter who
is responsible for the troubles of Folly Down? Then there is the
life of nature, self-contained, apart from man; the leaves will
not fall to suit the convenience of the sweeper:

> Mr. Burt approached one of the trees and angrily
> shook a bough that had a few leaves upon it. He hoped
> that this tree, at least, would permit him to finish with
> it. But not a leaf fell.
> 'They be only waiting till I be busy in they gardens,
> the dirty cowards!' said Mr. Burt gloomily.

Luke Bird, the simple idealist, finds that the geese which he
would like to baptise have a 'hatred of religion', a 'contempt
for Christianity'. The relationship of Nature and art, primal
matter and civilisation, is referred to more than once:

> 'Michael,' said Mr. Weston, 'although I know the
> world had to be before its creation could be described,
> yet I trust you are not one of those who place nature
> before art.'
> 'Indeed I am not,' replied Michael.
> 'I am glad of it,' said Mr. Weston.

The variety of life, of Nature, seen and enjoyed and suffered
and pondered, is shaped into the work of art which is *Mr.
Weston's Good Wine*. The omnipresent wine unifies all. The
language, easily collocating familiar and solemn, comic and
transcendental, is beautifully controlled to dramatic, ironic,
'atmospheric' ends. The wonderful conclusion of the book

E

again reminds one of *The Tempest* or *A Winter's Tale* in the way
it gathers strands together and culminates in a certain rich
relief and establishes a kind of peace. The Rev. Grobe, after
long, gentle, Godless mourning for his young and playfully
loving wife, is dead; Tamar having been embraced by Michael
in the 'salvation of love', is dead; Mrs. Vosper, the malicious
pimp, is dead. Luke Bird has been happily united to Jenny.
The Mumby boys, terrified by the opening of Ada's grave and
the lion's tramping, have come chastened (but not really
changed) to her sisters, Ann and Phoebe. Landlord Bunce has
decided, with a wink, that it is Mr. Weston who has done all
the mischief. The clock has started going again at the Inn. It is
after ten, and nervous Mr. Meek has been led homeward by
Grunter. Squire Mumby and Mr. Kiddle have also left to
continue their bargain talk in Kiddle's parlour:

> Mr. Weston's car had passed the inn in a moment
> and as rapidly reached the summit of Folly Down hill.
>     Once there, however, a curious grating sound was
> heard in the bowels of the car; the engine stopped, and
> the lights went out. Upon the hill there was complete
> darkness.
>     'The darkness pleases you, Michael,' said Mr.
> Weston in a gentle tone.    'I would that it pleased me
> too, but alas! you know well enough, the darkness and
> the light are both alike to me. Michael, do not be
> unhappy. You delighted Tamar—and she died . . .
>     'Ah!' said Mr. Weston, 'the new wine mourneth,
> the vine languisheth, all the merry-hearted do sigh.
> Remember, Michael, the writing upon the Indian
> loadstone that was as big as an Egyptian bean, and
> was hung in the temple of the priestess Bacbuc—
> "All things tend to their end" .'
>     Mr. Weston sighed. He turned towards Folly Down.
> The dawn was near. A lantern, a moving star, lit a
> carter's way from his cottage to Mr. Mumby's stable;
> a wakeful cock crew; the pleasant scent of wood smoke

was in the air, and the clatter of a well-bucket was heard.

'We have forgotten Miss Nancy Gipps,' exclaimed Mr. Weston. 'She was the first, except for those rude children, who noticed us.'

'What made you remember her, sir?' asked Michael.

'I think I hear her voice,' replied Mr. Weston, 'praying to me.'

'Does she ask for wine?' enquired Michael.

'No, only for a husband,' Mr. Weston answered.

'She is a woman,' observed Michael.

'Yes,' said Mr. Weston, 'and it's time she was married, and she shall have the mayor.'

'There is still your old enemy to be thought of,' remarked Michael. 'Have you forgotten him as well as Miss Gipps?'

'I certainly had,' replied Mr. Weston, 'but don't you think he would like to be a serpent again—a smaller adder?'

'I fancy,' said Michael 'that he would prefer to disappear in his own element—fire.'

'And so he shall,' cried Mr. Weston. 'Will you be so kind, Michael, as to drop a burning match into the petrol tank?'

'And we?' asked Michael.

'Shall vanish in the smoke,' replied Mr. Weston.

'Very well,' said Michael sadly.

Michael did as he was told. In a moment a fierce tongue of flame leaped up from the car; a pillar of smoke rose above the flame and ascended into the heavens. The fire died down, smouldered, and went out.

Mr. Weston was gone.

The silencing of the car, the darkness and Mr. Weston's gentle manner and gentle moralising, the dawn noises, the consideration given to the wants of Miss Gipps as to Mr. Weston's old enemy the devil, Michael's sad respect, the Biblical tongue of flame and pillar of smoke which ascended into the heavens, make up that effect above suggested, of relief and peace, an effect curiously like that of the beautiful words of the Duke in *Measure for Measure:*

> . . . Look, the unfolding star calls up the shepherd.
> Put not yourself into amazement how these things
> should be; all difficulties are but easy when they are
> known . . . Come away; it is almost clear dawn.

Without insisting on further possibilities of comparison, it can justly be said that *Mr. Weston's Good Wine* is among the finest of those 'novels as dramatic poems' which hold more of the English body and spirit, more essential Englishness than any other *genre* since Jacobean times. And for those who may not care to consider Powys a novelist at all, as not providing a sufficient wealth of 'realistic' character and fact, there is the choice between allegorist and fabulist. But considering what a variety of writers come under the term 'novelist' it would seem that Powys is most satisfactorily included among them.

*Chapter Four*

# FABLES AND SHORT STORIES

To say that T. F. Powys is among our great short story writers is to say that his finest achievements in this *genre* engaged his full creative energies. They are an expression, subtly and movingly presented, of certain profound interests and preoccupations, and a reader who doesn't approach them with a set expectation of the conventional short story ingredients and methods can hardly fail to be struck by their power and originality. Of the hundred or so short stories that Powys wrote, the fables and a few others, perhaps some thirty works in all, have the quality we hint at when we speak of fineness and permanence. Many of the rest are in one way or another attractive and interesting, and quite a number are very small affairs.

*Fables* appeared two years after *Mr. Weston's Good Wine;* that is, in 1929. (They were reprinted with the title, *No Painted Plumage*, in 1934). Mr. Louis Wilkinson has told how Llewelyn Powys suggested to his brother that he should 'write about anything; write about that log of wood and that old boot'. And though this advice was not the origin of the *Fables* in anything but a superficial sense—origin lies far back and deep in a writer's experience—it may well have been the immediate occasion which encouraged Powys to utilise his 'fancy' with relevance and point, to make it subserve his deepest inspirational purpose. Certainly we sense, irrespective of their themes and outlook, an absorbed enjoyment in the writing of these fables; to charge them with whimsy would be off the point. The mood is in fact that of the assured creativity of the artist.

The fables conform to what we understand as such, in that feelings and speech and actions are given to animals and inanimate things, and the narratives and interactions and dialogues become ways of presenting human situations. But no simple moral of the Æsop kind is to be drawn from them. It is not the conclusions that count but the full liberating and widening effect (as in, say, *Volpone*, or *Middlemarch* or *St. Mawr*) of the interplay of various feelings and attitudes, the pattern of humour, irony, anger, warm affirmation, wit gentle or sardonic. We are made to feel the wisdom of avoiding simple comprehensive judgments. Issues which may at first appear simple are shown to be delicate and ambiguous. In listening to discussion between a tombstone and a skull, between a withered leaf and a green one, between a hassock and a psalter, our sympathies and assent are likely to veer from one to the other and are often not settled even by the final, seemingly clinching episode, the smashing of the skull, the (green) leaf blown off in the storm, the burning of the hassock. The moral effect of the fables lies in their art: by their incident and dialogue, by the finely sustained tone, they move, invigorate, and enlighten. They add up to a humane vision of life, rendered with beauty and power.

*The Corpse and the Flea*—one of those fables, like *The Spittoon and the Slate*, *The Blind Hen and the Earthworm*, with a title slightly unpleasant to the conventional palate—has humanity, beauty, and a certain disturbing power. Faced with it or indeed with almost any of the others, the critic is between the devil of over-lengthy exposition, because he cannot take for granted any very wide knowledge of the fables in his readers, and the deep blue sea of the fear of leaving anything out, because these fables are tightly organised and the temptation to quote and quote is strong. Ultimately the flow and the full pattern can only be got from the creative original.

A middle-aged gentleman chanced to die at Madder in a little cottage bedroom near to the hill.

He was fifty. His life hadn't been as happy as it might and he ended his days by means of a chill that followed a long cough, at a quarter to six by the church clock, one pleasant September afternoon.

That is how *The Corpse and the Flea* opens, the surface-simplicity containing an unobtrusive concern for the undistinguished 'middle-aged gentleman' of fifty whose life 'hadn't been as happy as it might': the writing is cool, the killing cough is assimilated to the 'pleasant September afternoon'. Mr. Johnson's death was hardly noticed in the village.

The usual proceedings that follow a human death happened to this poor man. His body was washed with the rude care that is bestowed on one who cannot complain, his eyes were closed and pennies were placed upon them, his jaw was bound up until it stiffened, he was lifted into his coffin and his relations came to look at him.

Powys knows about death, it isn't horror to him, no 'attitude' rises from any emotional proclivity. On the night before the funeral, the dead man breathes again and looks about him:

A curtain had been drawn across the bedroom window, yet this curtain was so thin and torn that it did nothing to prevent a stream of moonlight from entering the room, the harvest moon being at that midnight hour full in the sky.

The atmosphere is one of peace with richness: the moonlight 'streams', the moon is the 'harvest' moon. Death is going to give Mr. Johnson, as a reward for 'the trouble of opening his eyes and ears for a little while again among the living', the power of understanding 'what the little creatures, who lived with him in his bedroom, might have to say for themselves'.

The night was silent and still; the moon hung high over the bare upland fields and shone richly upon the great corn stacks that belonged to Farmer Told.

In the cool solitudes of the country night there moved those large influences out of which a beauty comes that is so clear and holy that it would ease men —did they but inwardly mark it—from many a daytime fret. But this stillness that could give so good a peace out of doors was now broken by a cunning fox who, taking the chance of the hour, trotted across the gleaming fields, and, entering warily Mr. Told's stackyard, snatched at and carried off a plump cockerel that was foolish enough to go to roost upon the shaft of a wagon.

'Daytime fret' can be eased by the 'large influences' of 'clear and holy' beauty; but even amid the beauty there can be danger. The fox incident prevents a complacency in idealism. The first insect to speak is the death-watch beetle, whom the dead man's relations in their hurry to rifle the effects have shaken from a wardrobe. He is indignant at his upset and at the idea that his tapping is a mating-call:

'How could such loose behaviour,' the beetle exclaimed, 'come from one who has learned all the goodness of a cupboard where Sunday clothes have always hung, and from where, as everyone knows, my tapping, and that of all my ancestors, who have been heard from the commencement of the world, are the supernatural warnings that Death gives to the simple before it is too late, so that all who hear may make their peace with God and woo our blessed Saviour.'

Loose behaviour, Sunday clothes, the age and everlastingness of the sound, the superstition and the simple pious hope, and warning, all woven easily into one sentence. The beetle is followed by a large black female spider, crying out in rage upon the village nurse who, after failing to find anything of

value in the death-room, in temper sweeps down the cobweb
'that was the grandest of mansions to a simple spider':

> 'A fine bother I had,' cried the spider, 'to make all
> out of my own body, and then to have my web utterly
> broken and spoiled by an old witch, who only used
> her cursed cleanliness because she feared that Mr.
> Potten, the sexton, would add "slut" to "whore"
> when he spoke to her!'

When the spider wishes Mr. Johnson's corpse in hell for being
the cause of the disaster, he smiles, for if there is a hell, why
not a heaven too? Though he has always considered that hope
'an extremely unlikely one'. Mr. Johnson is now 'in a dreamy
state of peaceful expectation':

> . . . and as the night was warm, and the coffin,
> though cheap, was not uncomfortable, he was well
> content to remain in it.

But after a while he is startled to hear 'a still small voice' coming
from his shroud, 'which was indeed but his oldest and most
worn week-day shirt'. He thinks it may be his soul, which has
partly escaped and is lingering to have 'a half-hour's gossip
with its old friend and companion'. Having been poor all his
life, and hence without many friends, he is astonished and
gratified by the kind words he hears:

> 'You are my benefactor,' said a little soft voice.
> 'You are my dear friend upon whose blood I have
> reared grateful families. You, contrary to the custom
> of your race—unless you be gipsies or Indians—have
> ever permitted me to remain in comfort, hiding
> amongst your clothes. You have never tried to cast
> me from you with evil words, and, when I have bit
> you, you have only remarked, with a little shake of
> your body, that a small bite was a pleasure compared
> to the sneers and revilings of those old friends who
> had pretended to love you.'

The flea points out Mr. Johnson's desertion by all; but promises
not to leave him comfortless in his soul's 'long flight none knows

whither'. Mr. Johnson, 'touched to the heart by the insect's loving expressions', is moved to thankfulness and a kind of statement of belief and behaviour:

> 'One could not expect—for God Himself in His infinite mercy has set bounds to human love—that any one of my relations could be found whose love for me would so move them as to make them desire to go with me into the grave. And yet a little love—were it only enough to fill an empty snail's shell—can soothe and help the dying. But why should I complain or think myself ill-used, for the vast river of life that is black and foul with the tumult of lust and greed must on, and to belong to it must ever bring woe to a man. I have broken with the will that begot me and with the desires that made me. But I have wished ill to none. I have endeavoured to pacify, with meek words, all who have objected to my way of living, and though I may have failed to live virtuously, I have never meant to hurt anyone.'

In that speech the tone adequate to the condition where love is retained in the face of the recognition of truths which might embitter and harden, is beautifully caught and maintained. Humility, love, clear insight into evil, solemn renunciation of life, quiet self-justification, are all present. The talk turns to Mr. Johnson's brother, George, who, a fine gentleman and mayor of the town, is ashamed of his poverty-stricken brother, and with this talk Mr. Johnson finds he 'has a mind even now to live a little longer':

> He began to look lovingly about the cottage bedroom. There, by the side of the bed, was the chest of drawers that he knew so well, with one broken knob and a drawer missing, that he had given to a poor woman whose baby needed a cradle. A cracked looking-glass was upon the chest of drawers, and nailed to the wall was a text that a child had given him. Betty, the cat, that he was so fond of, was no

longer there, for when Mr. Johnson became sick he destroyed his cat with his own hands, so that she should neither suffer hunger nor be stoned by the rude children.

The indulgence in reminiscence (not all of it pleasant) of the everyday-domestic is followed, with a change of tone, by the flea's news of two more of Mr. Johnson's brothers who have better things to do than to sorrow for him. And as he smiles faintly he hears the insects again:

'Drat that ugly nurse!' cried the spider.
'Remember, remember your end,' the death-watch beetle tapped out melodiously.

Further memories come; the loss of his life is now regretted. The writing is gently and aptly sentimental as the past is dwelt upon, and common things take on an extraordinary value:

Mr. Johnson grew sadder. His thoughts now left the little room and wandered, for the last time, into the fields and the lanes. He had come—and the more he was forsaken by man the further he went in this way—to dote upon these common fields and simple hedgerows, where a little mouse might rustle the dead leaves and a fern grow . . .

His cat was not there. She used to clamber up the ivy outside his cottage and leap through the open window into his room and awaken him of a morning. There were other things, too, besides Betty, that he would never see again. The May daisies would be as lovely as ever when the next spring came, but he would be under the ground. Such sweet things as March celandines, and the coy roses that appear so daintily, and all of a sudden, upon the hedges in June, he would see them no more. Neither would he ever again walk to the copse down the green lane and hear the patter of ripe September nuts when the east wind blows. Never again would he carry in from his woodshed the winter logs to gladden his lonely

heart by their bright burning of a Christmas Eve.
Never more would he enjoy to lie warm in bed of a
frosty night when the owl passes under the moon,
followed by its shadow.

The inexorability of loss, pondered with love, is felt in the
repetitions and the persuasive rhythms; but the nostalgic
dream cannot last. He 'lets these thoughts go', and hears the
beetle warning the spider against making a web in the coffin
where they will screw her in with the 'bones'; the beetle
advises her to attach herself, not to Harold the house-decorator
brother, but to James, because 'he's the dirtier'. The dreams
of the past are quite shattered by that talk, and the end is near.
The story concludes thus:

> The insects ceased to talk and all the house was still.
>
> A change, a languor, came over Mr. Johnson, as
> though all his body was become utterly tired of
> living. A sound sleep from which there would be no
> waking was all that he wished for now. He settled him-
> self again in the bottom of the coffin.
>
> 'Forsaken,' he murmured mournfully, 'forsaken by
> a flea.'
>
> 'You are wrong,' said the little voice again, 'for I
> am still with you.'
>
> 'I am willing to die', murmured Mr. Johnson, 'but
> I do not wish that you should die too. I have a mind
> to die, but you, dear flea, must leap out of the coffin,
> and on to the bed, for the moon has sunk below
> Madder Hill, and the Dawn is near.'
>
> 'By no means,' replied the flea, 'shall I do what
> you ask. I wish to die as well as yourself—I will be
> with you always.'
>
> The shadow of a figure passed over the coffin, with
> arms outstretched.
>
> Mr. Johnson sank into unconsciousness.

The beauty and the peace are not only a matter of atmosphere
and of kindly feeling. What is conventionally a source of horror

or unpleasantness has been absorbed. The flea's words 'I will be with you always', are of course Christ's, as was previously its phrase, 'I will not leave you comfortless'; 'the shadow of a figure' is Christ, with arms outstretched to embrace, bless, and gather in (the Crucifixion suggests itself too); the shadow is also the Angel of Death, likewise blessing with *its* peace. As dawn comes to the world that still goes on outside the walls of the coffin where he lies, Mr. Johnson sinks quietly into the 'Dawn' of death. And there is a further profoundly enriching association: the flea is 'Good Deeds' to Johnson's 'Everyman'. It will be remembered that following the famous words spoken by Knowledge—'I will go with thee in thy most need, To go by thy side'—Everyman is forsaken by Beauty, Strength, Discretion, Five Wits:

> Everyman:    O Jesu, help! All hath forsaken me.
> Good Deeds:   Nay, Everyman; I will bide with thee.
>      I will not forsake thee indeed;
>      Thou shalt find me a good friend at need . . .
>      Beauty, Strength and Discretion do man forsake,
>      Foolish friends, and Kinsmen, that fair spake—
>      All fleeth save Good Deeds, and that am I.

And after Everyman has sunk into his grave, the Angel says 'Thy reckoning is crystal-clear'. Friends and relatives forsake Johnson too, and even those who seemed to be with him are not really with him; but he, Johnson-Everyman, is not deserted by the living reminder of the good deeds he has done throughout life. The way in which Johnson's soul is composed to meet death is unmistakably the work of a man who has re-lived *Everyman;* re-lived the traditional wisdom of which the play is a crystallisation. Moreover it is astonishing that Powys could re-live it so largely in its own idiom, while renewing it in his own intensely individual modification. It matters little whether what we have here comes from direct literary influence or from absorbed traditional wisdom, or from both. The important thing is that the tradition did reach Powys; and it was in a

highly sophisticated spirit (we may think of Bunyan too) that
he raised the idiom of it into art.

In *John Pardy and the Waves* we have something of the same
pattern of theme and feelings as in *The Corpse and the Flea:* the
man who is a nonentity and poor, the love of life, the cruelty
and coldness of respectable relatives, the release of death; there
is a similar everyday realism mingled with eloquence, a similar
acceptance and harmonising in the style:

> But John had no business to go about, other than the
> finding of a home for himself, and so he walked along
> the lanes and the byways where the loveliest flowers
> grew, resting now and then to scratch his sores, some
> of which had healed over.

John Pardy, however, is not Mr. Johnson, and the story has
what is usually called a 'bitter' (though perfectly controlled)
conclusion. The lazy, sponging, kind, simple-minded old man,
who has lived all his life enjoying the sunshine when he could
and always naïvely believing in men's goodness, despite many
experiences of men's baseness, having at the last been badly
treated by his relatives thinks he may find happiness in counting
the waves of the sea. Powys gives eloquent speech to the waves:

> 'We have lived, Mr. Pardy, for so long in our own
> eternal beauty, we have rocked for years without
> number the towering icebergs and the great ships,
> we have made sport for the sea-serpent and the
> monstrous whales, and we have rolled lazily in the
> wide empty spaces where God lives.'

But it is characteristic that Powys should also suggest that they
are at times lonely and weary of their mightiness: sometimes
they have

> 'crept inshore to see what was a-doing, approaching
> the shallows of the Bay of Weyminster in little
> inquisitive wavelets. There we have made merry with
> the bare feet of children, the rinds of bananas and the
> little paper tickets that are given to the holiday
> makers who hire the summer chairs.'

However, they are knowledgeable and concisely explanatory of the conduct of Mr. Pardy's brothers and sister. Mr. Pardy watches with pleasure and excitement an oncoming wave, describing it as it breaks, thinking it has died like a man, and will no more be seen:

> 'You are wrong' said the waves, 'for as soon as it broke and was gone, it became one with the vast waters of all the oceans. In a few million of years, perhaps—and what are these years to us?—those drops of water will collect again, rise up, roll on, and break upon the coast of Greenland during a summer night—but no human creature will see them . . . Our great joy comes when we break, yours when you are born, for you have not yet reached that sublime relationship with God which gives the greatest happiness to destruction.'

We are made to feel in the last few lines of the story, with their sudden change of direction in the waves' thoughts, the shock of their complacency in destructiveness, and that Mr. Pardy's kindness and trust, worn down at last by the years, have changed in this moment to despair, bitterness, and hate; nevertheless when he commits suicide all is dissolved:

> 'I am interested in what you say,' said John Pardy, 'and I have half a mind to join in your revels; but tell me, if I come to you shall I have the same pleasure in destroying others, as I am likely to have when I am destroyed myself?'
>
> 'You may sink a ship,' answered the waves, 'and with good luck you may become a tidal wave that will drown a city.'
>
> John Pardy walked into the sea.

The utter loss of hope, the terrible finality of the decision ultimately made on those particular grounds, is felt through the succession of emotionless statements.

Life, beauty, evil, love, death: out of the contemplation emerges a remarkable pattern and balance of interests and feelings, and a poise which is wisdom. In *The Stone and Mr. Thomas* the intense appreciation of lived actualities is balanced with a no less complete knowledge of annihilation and oblivion. The skull of Mr. Thomas, lying upon a rubbish-heap, in an argument with his gravestone will not believe that he, who enjoyed so much, is forgotten:

> 'What of those peaceful days that I spent in rowing my little boat under the white cliffs? Are they gone so early? I behold now the dark blue colour of the sea, so rich, so heavy, while above the hot lustful sun ravished all comers with its love. Did not the beauty of those summer days sink deep within me, when the sea-weed, far down in the dark colour of the water, moved here and there swaying delicately, with so fantastic a loveliness, that a man's soul could melt in the very beauty that the eyes saw? . . .

> 'I walked out again in the same mood, and the winter fields were all become the same colour as my mind: not gaudy with the greedy wantonness of summer, but with the grey colour of peaceful delights. The silence I walked in grew kinder, grew more gentle—large snowflakes were falling. The peace I moved in grew upon me, a gracious resignation filled my mind, for now all my daring summer days had found a winter's nest to lie in, safe and hidden. The earth caressed me, the quiet came that numbs the rude and releases the golden numbers of soft music— can it be that I am now forgotten, I, who remember so well?'

The stone is unmoved by all the 'fine talk'; it alone will last. In the end the poor skull is reduced to admitting the futility of his former life. But the homely confident tone of the stone, while utterly and unfeelingly nullifying the pretensions of the skull, and virtually negating his being, nevertheless contains the suggestion, unexpected but spontaneous, of new life and usefulness in 'excellent cool dung for spring onions':

' . . . All would have been well had I been nothing, had I never been born!'

'Then all will be well now,' replied the gravestone carelessly—'for Tom Platter told Sexton Potten that old bones well crushed with a beetle make an excellent cool dung for spring onions. That is the reason why Mr. Potten has cast upon the rubbish-heap a few of the remains of the bones of men. He now wishes to try the effect of this useful manure.

'This very night he is wheeling his barrow here— he is now in the churchyard path—and you, Mr. Thomas, will be the first to be shovelled in. He takes you up and examines you. He thinks that you were once Old Barker who, when in drink, was found drowned in Farmer Told's horse-pond.'

When Powys reduces pretensions, when he puts egocentricity and the over-grand and the inflated into perspective, it is rarely that mockery is the sole or chief impulsion. His dealings with solemnities real or factitious are more often than not touched or suffused with a compassionate humour; there is a quiet regardfulness for all forms of life, a concern for the moderate pleasures of everyday. *Mr. Pim and the Holy Crumb* deals with God and Holy Communion in a manner which should move and delight faithful and unbeliever alike. The 'wonderful story'—how ironical is the phrase?—of the 'transformation of God into the Holy Bread', has been told by the clergyman for the first time to Mr. Pim, the church clerk, ex-rabbit-trapper and ploughman. He thinks hard about it, and after mentioning to two old women how

'the Lord God, the Creator of the world, who be named
  Christ by drunken people when pub do close, do change
'Isself into they scrimpy bites of Mr. Johnson's bread
  that thee do take and eat up at church railings,'

and after an encounter with the genteel Miss Pettifer, he decides to speak about it to his dead friend, John Toole, who had been a poor man like himself:

F

As Miss Pettifer, however late she came, had always to be allowed time to adjust her veil, sprinkle a little scent upon her handkerchief, and kneel down, Pim had no need to hurry back to the church. With his hands still behind his back, he bent over the grave.

'John,' said Pim, 'I've a-heard something that must make 'ee laugh—'tis that God Almighty in our little church do change 'Isself into a bite of stale bread.'

'That be a tale,' replied a muffled voice from the ground: 'but what be weather doing up above?'

'There be snowflakes a-falling as large as feathers,' replied Pim, showing no surprise because his friend spoke so lowlily, 'as large as feathers, but they do melt on ground.'

'So I did fancy,' replied the buried John; 'but now I've somewhat to ask of 'ee that b'aint about the weather.'

'Ask away, Johnnie,' replied Pim.

'If 'ee do happen,' said the muffled voice, 'to get a word wi' thik crumb of bread that be the Lord on High, ask 'E to be kind enough to look over Johnnie Toole at the last day, for I be well content to bide where I be now. There b'aint no work to do here and all be ease and comfort, and many a merry story do we bones tell together.'

Pim sighed. He nodded twice at the grave, turned and walked to the church . . .

John's words have their effect. Mr. Pim, humble, unambitious, direct, converses on equal terms with the Crumb that has dropped from his bread at his first Communion in the wintry church. He stands for a commonsense acceptance of death and a feeling of the continuity of rural life and of oneness with the earth he knows:

'A well-dug grave be good and a coffin be pretty, but I haven't a fancy for neither heaven nor hell. I've a mind to bide where I be put same as Johnnie, while

above, in village, days will pass and be gone, will
return again and be gone. Thik grey stone that do bide
out in field will still be there, and maybe Mr. Told's
barn will bide about too. Johnnie and I don't want to
go to no new place, we'd sooner be dry bones in
Madder—for 'tis our home—than lords in heaven.'
In the continuation of the interchange Powys's gift of fusing
profound and simple into a harmonious view and feeling is
beautifully shown; shrewdness and life-reverence mingle:

'But every one else wants to rise again,' remarked
the Crumb, 'even the clergy.'

'Clergymen,' observed Pim, ' b'aint easily satisfied.
They do keep servants, and often a little dog. They do
eat mutton and rice pudding, stretch out their legs
before the fire and listen to music being played.'

'Say,' inquired the Crumb, 'do people ever talk
about me here? Do they name me at all?'

'Thee's name be useful,' murmured Pim.

'For what?' asked the Crumb.

'Shepherd do shout Thee's name to 'is dog,
Carter Beer do damn wold Boxer wi' Thee, and Mr.
Tucker do say Thee b'aint no liar.'

'And yet I made the green grass, Mr. Pim!'

' 'Tis plain Pim with the clergy,' remarked the clerk.

"Mr. Pim!"

'Yes, Holy Crumb.'

'Mr. Pim, I am disappointed with you. I hoped you
would have wished to dwell with me, for, to tell you
a truth, I made heaven glorious for you and for
John Toole.'

'But Thee made the earth too, and the sweet mould
for our bed, and Thee'll have Miss Pettifer in heaven,
who be a lady.'

'But you, Mr. Pim, who have never eaten of the
tree of knowledge: I had a mind to be happy with
you for all eternity.'

'Ha! ha! ha!' laughed Pim, 'I do see the fix Thee be in. But b'aint 'Ee God?'

'Yes, alas so!'

'Then do 'Ee come and be a rotted bone by John and I. But allsame Thee needn't hurry I there. I have a mind to eat a spring cabbage at Easter.'

'Mr. Pim, Mr. Pim, you are exactly what I meant myself to be. When I consider the troubles I have caused,' said the Holy Crumb in a low voice, 'I almost wish I had entered into a mouse instead of a man.'

'Hist! hist!' whispered Pim, 'Thee may do thik now, for a mouse do live under altar table who do creep out when all's quiet.'

Pim moved to the front pew, winked at the Crumb and remained silent. A little mouse, with a pert prying look, crept out from under the altar and devoured the Holy Crumb.

The greatness of 'God' is not revoked: He made the green grass; and He is pitied for the burden of responsibility and blame He bears. But the Holy Crumb is also a crumb of the village baker's bread, helping to keep alive the creature which devours it without thought. And in the end the here and now of the spring cabbage is more to Mr. Pim than the promise of a 'glorious heaven'; though even here, the cabbage is an Easter one.

Sometimes a deliberate narrowing of attitude results in an irony of great force. Whereas in *Mr. Pim*, God, the Judgment Day, the altar, the men, the mouse, Holy Communion, scrimpy bites of bread, the grave, spring cabbage, are harmonised in a richly humane tone, *The Bucket and the Rope* has an ironic intensity born, as Swift's sometimes is, out of a casual-seeming manner which is actually the perfection of control. The rope, with the body of Mr. Dendy still hanging from it, and the bucket, lying on its side after being kicked from under his feet, discourse on the possible causes of Mr. Dendy's action. They wish to understand the ways of men. While the reader has readily guessed that the cause was the unfaithfulness of his wife, the bucket and the rope, basing their conversation on the normal happiness of Mr. Dendy's life and what they see as the kindness of Mrs. Dendy, suggest reason after callow reason: the one action of Mr. Dendy—a loving action—which they found unusual was this:

'Only once,' observed the bucket sadly, 'did I notice Mr. Dendy act in a way that was not usual for a village man. He was bearing me, full, along a path from a small cottage where he bought swill. On each side of the path there were flowers, both white and yellow. Mr. Dendy set me down, a rotten orange bobbed up on my surface. Mr. Dendy rested by the path, plucked some of the flowers, and seemed to take delight in holding them in his hand.'

'What did he do next?' asked the rope.

'He carried the flowers home to his wife,' replied the bucket.

As they are sensible talkers with some knowledge of the practicalities of country life, the horror that emanates from their utter ignorance of the emotions and the moral laws connected with human love and sexuality is the greater: the horror-in-humour is in their ingenuous floundering on and on. The magnificent end of the fable is given below; the rope has just explained how Mr. Dendy in his Sunday best (having been urged to go to church by his wife, Betty) hid behind a bundle of straw by a chink in the wall of the shed:

'For the pleasure of witnessing the kindness of his wife, I suppose,' said the bucket.

'One would have thought so,' replied the rope, 'but the look upon Mr. Dendy's face when he saw what was going on did not warrant such a supposition.'

'Perhaps he thought,' reasoned the bucket, 'that Betty should have remained at home and warmed the rabbit pie for his supper; for the sermon preached by Mr. Hayball always made him extremely hungry, and Betty was not to be expected to know that he was not at church. I have seen the pigs fed so often, and I know how hungry animals are, and as food keeps a man alive and prevents him from becoming a dead carcass, it is natural that a man should wish the woman that he keeps to prepare food for him, even though she may prefer to be loving and kind to another man.'

'You should have heard Mr. Dendy,' said the rope; 'he gnashed his teeth and moaned horribly, and when his wife's friend seemed to be altogether forgetting his sorrow, being come, as the lyric poet says, "Where comfort is—" Mr. Dendy crept out of the bundle and hid in the lane, snarling like a bitten dog.'

'His hunger, I suppose, had gone beyond the proper bounds,' suggested the bucket.

'It is difficult,' said the rope, after a few minutes' silence, as the body swung to and fro, 'for us to decide what could have troubled this good man. No one had robbed him. No one had beaten or hurt him, and never once since they had been married had Betty refused his embraces.'

'It must have been that nosegay,' exclaimed the bucket.

Controlled comic bitterness could hardly go further.

*The Spittoon and the Slate* has a climax more *overtly* savage than that of *The Bucket and the Rope*, which it resembles in being at least in part a treatment of sexuality. Both the spittoon and the slate worship the young girl Rosie, the publican's daughter, and cannot believe that God, the loving Father, has destined her to be enjoyed by Squire Budden, whose 'use is to destroy all that is lovely'. The last sentence of the story is this:

As soon as Squire Budden had finished with her, he staggered to the spittoon and spat.

The disgust with brutality is plain and intense, but it is controlled as an element of the whole. When we recall that the spittoon itself, an elegant one, had never before been used, that it had wondered what was its purpose in the world, that it had longed to have a purpose, that the slate had agreed with it in fancying that its fate was bound up with Rosie's, then that final stark sentence, damning to the man as it is, has an 'art-moral' effect immeasurably more powerful than any expression of mere disgust could be.

The fables, simple in a superficial sense—never an unusual and rarely a long word, never an involved sentence—and developing with plenty of external action and incident and lively dialogue—

'Mr. Keddle, sitting at his ease, would rub his hands, being glad that the quiet state of his mind permitted him still to enjoy the pleasant taste of his breakfast, that was followed by a pipe of mild tobacco. As he puffed at his pipe, that he always took with his last cup of coffee, he would look in an interested manner at the pan in which the porridge had been cooked.'

'Prithee, friend,' inquired the clout, 'was not the pan you?'

'How otherwise, if the pan were not I, could I have told you this tale?'

'You might have invented it,' replied the clout curtly.

'It would not be proper,' said the pan 'to prove an argument by fiction.'

'It was Plato's way,' remarked the clout.

'The more fool he!' cried the pan angrily.

'Be so good as to continue,' said the clout.

'Mr. Keddle,' went on the other, 'only looked to remind his wife that the pan was empty . . .'

the fables, simple-seeming, often work with a subtle interplay of viewpoints in a presentment of complexities. Both sides are

persuasive in the argument between the tombstone and Mr. Thomas; and though the last remaining portion of Mr. Thomas, namely the skull, is to be annihilated sooner than the stone, which appears to 'win', it is nevertheless Mr. Thomas who has had the intense and varied life. And a further dimension is given by the fact that both are egocentric: the skull believes that the bits of grit and soil ingrained in it are the finest pearls, and the stone believes that a cat who in sharpening his claws on it scratched off the moss, did so in order to admire the beauty of the lettering. Darkness finally gathers Nathaniel to it in *Darkness and Nathaniel*, and Nathaniel accepts, but we do not forget his previous horrors of the 'sameness' and the 'unchangeableness' that appertain to darkness, nor do we forget his love of light: 'He loved light, he called light his friend, he loved colour. He was happy when the sky was blue . . . '
Pity for the hen in *The Blind Hen and the Earthworm* turns to amusement at the pride it develops, until its head is suddenly dashed against the gardener's boot, while the worm, which it had been relentlessly seeking to devour, sinks into the mould. Often the human characters are ambiguously attractive or otherwise. John Pardy's relatives treat him abominably. We are to sympathise with him; but we are also to ask how we ourselves should behave towards him in similar circumstances. He is likeable and helpless. But he is also a hopeless, sponging misfit. Nowhere in the fables are we invited to make easy final judgments. Out of a conventional subject, from which, without being adverted we should expect a setting-out of fairly plain issues, remarkable and beautiful complexes are made. What, for instance, would seem at first to be simply a dichotomy of viewpoints in *The Withered Leaf and the Green*, becomes a richly artistic pattern with subtle variations of feelings clustered around such ideas as the bliss of the senses, naïve but intense love of, and trust in, life, knowledge with disenchantment, the beauty of the adder which kills the child, the childish greed of an old man, the breaking of illusions, the conception of happiness. All these are delicately dealt with in incident,

description, dialogue with its tones of voice and gestures. In a
true sense the fables are prose-poems: by organisation, not by
purple writing.

The remaining eighty-odd of Powys's short stories are not
fables; almost all of these are very short. With a few exceptions,
they could fairly readily be grouped into categories: humorous,
serious-moral, whimsical, pathetic, sentimental-melodramatic,
allegorical-supernatural, horror.

On the whole, although Powys's humour finds felicitous
expression over and over again, the lighter stories are the
weaker. Too often the story is a mere elaboration of a fancy,
as when by the fixing of a weather-cock to show North a couple
are enabled to marry, because the girl's father hates the North
wind and will not venture out even to stop the wedding he
disapproves of. These stories tend to be two-dimensional only.
The presence of a moral in them isn't enough to give depth.
Sometimes a kind of mock-moral runs through the narrative to
produce pleasant and amusing effects: sexton Truggin teaches
Farmer Hoard a lesson for his cupidity by wheeling him, when
he is dead-drunk, on the bier into the church, and when he
wakes, terrifying him into repentance with the requisite
macabre and solemn effects.

In some of the stories the moral is less illustrated than integral,
and this is so because genuine feeling, even though without any
very great strength or depth, accompanies the small, neatly
executed structure of character, event, and sometimes symbol.
In *Jane Mollet's Box*, for instance, there is something more than
fanciful embroidering of a common Christian-virtue theme.
The Rev. Gasser, bereaved of his wife and unhappy, succumbs
eventually to a sense of failure and damnation. He has had for
a long time a large picture of St. Peter in his study. He now
covers with a screen the keys in the picture; there will be no
entrance into Heaven for him. The young girl Jane, who does
some work for him, is distressed by his condition, and goes for
advice to Mr. Vardy, the Voltaire-reading cobbler. Mr. Vardy
tells her that he doesn't suppose St. Peter's are the only keys in

the world; he tells her too that one sometimes gives away what
one loves—'it has been done, you know'; and Jane, after going
the round of the ironmongers in Weyminster, knocks at Mr.
Gasser's door at the moment when he is going to hang himself,
and holds out the sea-shell-covered box he had given to her
when she was a child:

> ' 'Tis thee's birthday present I have brought,' she
> cried, 'for Mr. Vardy do say it be only what I love best
> that will save 'ee from Hell.'

> Jane held out the box; Mr. Gasser received it into
> his hands. Jane was gone.

> Mr. Gasser carried the box into his study. He would
> leave it there, pray a little for Jane, and then return
> to the woodshed. The box was heavy. When Mr.
> Gasser put it down, there was a clink of metal inside.

> Mr. Gasser opened the box. It was full of keys.

> He turned them out upon the table. There were
> keys of all shapes and sizes, from a great cottage-
> key to the smallest key for a modern lock.

> Mr. Gasser covered his face and wept.

> He returned the screen to the fire.

The story ends thus, with Mr. Gasser saved by the child's love.
These particular stories seem to me to be just on the credit side
of sentimentality. Without great force, they nevertheless
impress with a certain warmth and a certain sharpness of
statement. This sharpness, effectively employed for narrative
and simple dramatic purposes in a number of Powys's short
stories (in some, the material and intention being so slight, it is
little more than a mannerism) is not of course the same thing
as the compactness and pregnant economy of the fables proper.
It is nonetheless original and remarkable. *Lie Thee Down,
Oddity!* with its significance of contrast between lawn and heath,
its Mr. Cronch who obeys his profound impulse to do good
though he knows the dangers of so doing in a world organised
as ours is, its suggestive touches of description, its skilful
juxtaposing of social wrongs with Mr. Cronch's actions—he is

unsanctimonious like Christ—is one of several realistic-allegorical stories whose excellence depends largely upon that concise manner. In this connection *Uriah on the Hill*, *What Lack I Yet?* and *The Dewpond* come to mind.

Extreme instances of greed and cruelty—cruelty in particular—and of terror and anxiety, make up the material for Powys's purely 'horror' stories. They are without any Poe-like luridness, but whether they are direct-overt accounts or skilful structures of ironies and innuendoes, they can be classed 'horror' because of their intensity. They all have, it seems to me, a basis of psychological truth even though the facts of the story are on occasions like those of the most highly-coloured and bizarre occurrences reported in the most sensational newspapers. They are real enough to be shocking, especially to those who believe that there are certain things about human nature that are best left unrecognised. The proportion of ostriches among those who read Powys is likely to be very small, though it can be admitted that if a man spent his writing-life predominantly on works of this kind he would be stamped as narrow, unfree, sombre, obsessed. Powys never forgot the force and incidence of human depravity of the darkest kind, but the short stories dealing exclusively with that are very few, perhaps half a dozen.

Mr. Meek, mole-catcher and devout church-goer, catches a mole to bake alive as a cure for his wife's cancer. He wishes to save her because she is a good mole-skinner. She dies, but he still bakes the mole, with his boy Jimmy an interested spectator; this is how the story ends:

> Mr. Meek placed the mole upon the table and admired it.
>
> ' 'Tis a pity,' he said, 'to spoil 'is coat, but what be the use of a woman who do only stay and groan, and don't skin no moles.'
>
> As if in answer to Mr. Meek, a groan that sounded like her last came from Mrs. Meek, who lay upstairs.
>
> Mr. Meek told Jimmy to look to the mole and went to his wife. That groan had been her last. Mr. Meek

returned to the kitchen and watched the fat mole that Jimmy was playing with.

'Mole do fancy,' said Mr. Meek, smiling, 'that now Sarah be dead, I be going to be kind and let the cat 'ave 'im.'

Jimmy pointed to the oven.

Mr. Meek smiled.

*The Baked Mole*, which is a good minor story, is grim, but it is not sadistic. Condemnation of cruelty need not be explicit; the felt horror in a story of this kind is a warrant of the writer's intention.

Selfishness, grossness, callousness, perverse sexuality, are portrayed in an astonishing short story called *The Barometer*. It is astonishing because of the force generated by the perfectly deliberate laconic unfolding of a vicious situation and action; nothing is commented on, the writer seems to be merely narrating and describing; but echoes and cross-references, odd facts and occurrences are seen finally to link up in the whole pattern. The pattern is not a big and rich one, and the range of feeling is narrow. But even when the manner of functioning of the barometer is known, and the identity of the pig, and the significance of certain things which at a first reading are likely to seem merely irrelevant, the duplicity and the completeness of the callousness continue to make themselves felt both in the structure and in the deadly detachment of the telling. The closeness of the organisation is such that quotation would not be helpful without a more complete exposition of the story than it is possible to offer here. If *The Barometer* fails to be a great short story it is because its concern is with a corner and not with a central node of human affairs. Perhaps its quality is best suggested by calling it a striking *tour de force*, where preoccupation with the human problem counts for less, if only a little less, than technique. There is not quite the fusion that is so perfect in the fables.

Several of the longer short stories, on the other hand, with deeply felt themes and containing magnificent passages, seem to me faulty technically, inclined to looseness and rambling.

The allegorical *When Thou Wast Naked*, for instance, despite the interest and the convincingness of the presentment of good-natured Mr. Priddle, and the odd charm of much of the incident, involving (say) snobbery, or social ambition, or modern rush, has too many Biblical analogies and too much barely-relevant material. There is some excellent writing, as when the source of the quite innocent Mr. Priddle's money is indicated—the Great War:

> Universal murder presented him with money. Blood and destruction politely gave to Mr. Priddle a modest fortune. Ruin and rape provided him with property. Sudden death gave him gold.

There are touches of ironical humour:

> ' 'E be a friend to drink and women, though,' said Mr. Coney, who always wished to do honour to the farmer's character.
>
> 'He always behaves like a gentleman,' remarked Charley, bravely.
>
> 'So 'e do,' replied Mr. Coney, 'if 'e do get a woman into old barn, where barrel of beer be kept for quiet drinking.'

And the conclusion, too lengthy to quote here, admirably suggests the trivial-minded worldliness of the gossipers as well as the pathos of the defeated and ruined Priddles. That the impression we have, notwithstanding our discovery of the (neat but not very significant) references to many details in Ezekiel XXIII and in spite of our seeing Mr. Priddle as another version, well presented, of that prophet—the Word of the Lord, but kindly and charitable—is one of pathos and not tragedy, perhaps indicates the general feeling-tone of this interesting tale.

We are not likely to dispute a tragic element in *The Only Penitent*. Not in the intention merely—the story is meant in itself to be tragic—but in achievement, especially in that represented by the conclusion. In the language of the last page or two is realised, with originality and dramatic force, a powerful sense of evil, death, and pity. Up till then Mr. Hayhoe has been treated with a gentle irony that is most often of the comic-sympathetic kind, and it may be felt that the power that finally comes to him is rather imposed from outside by the author than developed out of the experience he has been given in the story. Mr. Hayhoe is not King Lear. Nevertheless the naïveté of Mr. Hayhoe's belief in men's goodness and in their readiness to confess their sins, and his waiting vainly in the church, Sunday after Sunday, for the penitents to come, and the doubts that gradually invade him—

> Was all sin, then, a mere chimera, he wondered; only a folly of the mind and no burden at all? And was all religion a mess of sour pottage, and every minister only a falsehood, with a task sweetened for him with the rich sugar of a goodly stipend?

And then further:

> Was all life but a fantastic feast, where the worms fouled the platter, and death waits upon the guests?

the dejection, the self-condemnation, are, together with some humorous interludes, an interesting prelude to the superb dénouement, even though they do not amount to an experience forceful or complex enough to make the whole into the kind of parable of the growth of innocence into experience that the story aims at being. The final pages comprise description of a week of strange, sultry, disquieting weather, a great storm with thunder and lightning, some talk between Mr. Hayhoe and his ever-loyal wife Priscilla, and then his exchange with Tinker Jar. (Jar, who is often seen walking upon Madder Hill with his pack on his back, has been particularly loved by Hayhoe, who has even confessed his own small sins to him, and with benefit too, for Jar has lightly dismissed them: 'But though Mr. Jar can take away my troubles, he is very often sad himself.') Here is the last page and a half of this story of forty pages:

> 'Tinker Jar is coming now,' cried Priscilla, 'he is already in the church path. Oh!'—she stepped back into the church—'what a blinding flash! Surely the heavens opened, and he must be killed.'

'Go, Priscilla,' said Mr. Hayhoe, in an altered tone, when the crash of thunder was quieted, 'kneel down in your place, and hope that the sins of this penitent may be forgiven him, for, unworthy as I am, I know now that Mr. Jar is coming to confess to me.'

No sooner had Mr. Hayhoe said this than the thunder altogether ceased, and torrents of rain began to fall, as though all the windows of heaven had been opened.

Mr. Hayhoe stepped to his hiding-place, but, feeling that there was no need to put any barrier between himself and Tinker Jar, he folded the screen and laid it aside. Mr. Jar entered the church and approached the confessor, and without a word knelt humbly before him.

'Who are you?' asked Mr. Hayhoe, whose own voice sounded strange to him.

'I am the Only Penitent,' replied Jar. 'I have come to confess my sin to you.'

'Can I give you absolution?' asked Mr. Hayhoe, in a low tone.

'You can,' replied Jar, 'for only by the forgiveness of man can I be saved.'

'Can that be so?' asked Mr. Hayhoe.

'He who forgives a sin, loves the sinner,' answered Jar. 'By love, all is forgiven.'

'Dare I love you?' asked Mr. Hayhoe.

Jar bowed his head.

'I crucified my son,' he said. Mr. Hayhoe was silent. ' 'Twas I who created every terror in the earth, the rack, the plague, all despair, all torment. I am the one who rips up the women with child, every foul rape is mine act, all pain and all evil are created by me. Can you love me now?'

Mr. Hayhoe looked through the open vestry door, and saw Priscilla still kneeling.

'You have not told all,' he said. 'You have not

spoken of the joy and love that a woman can give,
you have not told of the great peace that you also can
bestow upon those who desire it. You have not told of
the joy of the young creatures whom you lead to the
dance in the green pastures.'

'I destroy all men with a sword,' said Jar. 'I cast
them down into the pit, they become nothing.'

'Hold!' cried Mr. Hayhoe. 'Is that last word true?'

'It is,' answered Jar.

'Then, in the name of Man,' said Mr. Hayhoe
boldly, 'I forgive your sin; I pardon and deliver you
from all your evil; confirm and strengthen you in all
goodness, and bring you to everlasting death.'

Whether we see Jar as the only person *good* enough to repent,
or whether we consider that he, as God, is responsible for all
men's actions and therefore only he needs to repent—I believe
both conceptions hold in this story—the pattern of feelings and
attitudes is finely developed as Hayhoe grows in strength until
he is 'bold', at the furthest point of his knowledge. His effort
to balance Jar's confession of 'all pain and all evil' with a
reminder of love, peace, and joy, fails because Jar follows up
with the certainty of annihilation. But after such a recital of
evils and pains, death is surely a release. That is why, finally,
Hayhoe can forgive God; He invented death. But the final
utterance is one of strength, not of surrender to 'cynicism'.
God is not only pardoned for evil, He is confirmed in 'all
goodness' until He too attains the blessing of 'everlasting
death'. (We remember Mr. Weston's desire to drink of his own
dark wine.) Hayhoe's disenchantment, the dark realisation
which does not however negate belief in a *possible* goodness,
and which makes him not weaker but stronger, finds its expression in a powerfully ironic adaptation of Prayer Book
language and rhythms and involves not only the overthrow
of a lifetime's hopes and beliefs but also the refusal to accept
at least the orthodox notion of the 'everlasting life' promised
by two thousand years of Christianity.

*Chapter Five*

# UNCLAY

UNCLAY was the last-published novel of T. F. Powys. He lived
for some twenty-two years after its publication in 1931, but he
wrote no more full-length novels. In many ways an
extraordinary and deeply interesting book, and quite clearly
the work of a distinguished mind by any standards, *Unclay*
misses the greatness which belongs to *Mr. Weston* and the
*Fables*. This claim for both its interest and its comparative
failure seems to me not over-difficult to substantiate, despite
the peculiarities of action and of character-delineation and the
ambivalences of attitude with which critic and general reader
have to contend.

The peculiarities are of course inherent in the convention
Powys works in, and usually they are either readily enough
accepted or seen to be indispensable elements of the complete
work. In *Unclay* the nature of many of the episodes and the fact
that the conception and treatment of the chief character,
Death, is quite original, make the 'strangeness' loom disturbingly large. And the strangeness is sometimes felt to be more
sensational than significant. The ambivalences, on the other
hand, come out frequently in explicit general statements, and
the confusion they are apt to suggest in the author is perhaps

G

a main reason for his failure to create another work of the
order of *Mr. Weston*. The frequent terseness of the generalisations (there are many of them, in quite lengthy sequences)
seems to indicate rather a forcing of attitude than any great
certainty from the centre.

John Death, having lost a parchment which contained God's
command to 'unclay' Joseph Bridle and Susie Dawe, spends
the summer at the village of Dodder. He rests from his everlasting labour of 'scything', and finds delight in love. In the end
Death accomplishes his tasks, and vanishes from the scene.
*Unclay* is yet another of Powys's stories that have for their
emphasised theme 'the two great realities, love and death'.
As soon as the parchment is found, John Death has to give up
love and resume his duties: there is a sense in which Love and
Death are irreconcilable enemies:

> A day passes and the evening comes, and we think
> to return, as Mr. Solly thought, to our garden of
> nuts—but, instead, we go elsewhere. To where an
> everlasting battle is fought between Love and Death.
> Can no shadow come between these two, or a
> fountain of water, or lonely silence?
> Will God never be still?

That almost all the situations and characters of *Unclay*
resemble or are identical with those of previous books is not a
simple matter of uncreative repetition. Certainly there are
many times when we register the comment, 'We have read this
before', but when we note also that the book makes incidental
references to people and things in earlier works, the clout and
the pan for instance, and the hassock and the psalter, and Mr.
Weston and old Barker and Luke Bird, then we realise that the
repetitions and echoes are quite intentional. Mr. Solly of
*Unclay* is much the same Mr. Solly as in *Innocent Birds*, more a
spectator and a commenter than an actor, kindly but timid;
the partnership of Dawe, miser and vicious father, and Mere,
the savagely sadistic farmer, recalls that of Charlie Tulk and
James Andrews in *Mark Only*, and also brings to mind Mew of

*The Left Leg;* Joe Bridle is like Mark himself in a certain
stupidity of heavy persistence in matters of love, and Susie
is like Mark's Nellie in her dissatisfaction with that kind of
love; Dady is a fly-crusher like Mr. Bugby; Lord Bullman is
here again; and so on. There is a factor, however, which makes
*Unclay* something quite distinct from a tired working-over of
old material ; this is the role of John Death. And a certain note
in the attitude towards love, heard often enough before in
Powys but not with such prominent and pervasive emphasis,
has the interest of vital creativity even though we may feel
bound to reject it as in some measure a retrogression from the
broad all-roundness of *Mr. Weston's Good Wine.*

John Death, though an extremely interesting and original
creation, cannot from the nature of his role represent the kind
of human centrality and wisdom that are supplied in the
figure of the wine-merchant. In the main he is confined to
carrying out God's—Tinker Jar's—commands to 'unclay', or
to warning grimly and often wittily of the death to come, and
to seeking love in the persons of several of the characters.
But in spite of this narrowed scope, Powys manages to make
him varied and human in his changes of mood, in his proneness
to human frailties as well as his easily exercised beneficences.
Actually though, it is precisely this rather casual variability
which, while making John Death delightful, also takes ultimately from his significance as a symbolical figure of the
profoundest kind.

He does, of course, make wholly serious claims for his work
on earth. Talking to Priscilla, the wife of Parson Hayhoe, he
speaks of the peace he brings and of his power over every
individual life from its very beginning:

> 'When a deathly numbness overcomes a body, when
> the flesh corrupts, and the colour of the face is
> changed in the grave, then I have done for a man
> more than love can do, for I have changed a foolish
> and unnatural craving into everlasting content.
>
> 'In all the love feats, I take my proper part. When

a new life begins to form in the womb, my seeds are
there, as well as Love's. We are bound together in
the same knot. I could be happy lying with you now,
and one day you will be glad to lie with me . . . '

His power as a warning and as an agent of terror is often
impressively suggested. There is the fine chapter called 'Strange
Music', where following a page about sounds—'As the years
move onward, sounds change. Sounds that used to be listened
to in older times are not heard now'—we are made to feel the
ominousness of the sound of the scythe being sharpened and its
effect on the drinkers at the Dodder Inn and on several other
characters. To Mr. Hayhoe, reading *The Watsons*,

the sound made a strange music; it became loud,
then soft. It grew angry. Stone upon steel, one could
almost see the sparks fly; wild fierce rage was in the
quick clash—utter destruction. Then, though the
sharpening continued, the sound was softened, while
around it, in some green meadow, the larks were
singing.

Again there came a steady rhythm, a continuous
note, and in this sound Mr. Hayhoe recognised the
quick passing of time, and the certainty of man's end:

(Mr. Hayhoe is moved to sigh that Jane Austen had not lived
longer: 'Oh! why had she not been permitted to write a few
more books!') The 'strange music' is followed by Mere's
attempt to assault Susie. As he was about to rush into her room,
someone outside in the lane laughed:

Mere went to the window. Being a rich man, he had
always been a careful one too. He did not like to be
made fun of. Whoever had laughed, had laughed at
him. But who in Dodder would have dared to do that?
The laugh in the lane had an odd quality about it;
it was the laughter of one who in an argument knew
that he would have the last word. There was no
respect shown to Mr. Mere in that laugh.

For one moment Mr. Mere was afraid. Then he

began to reason with himself, and decided that Susie could wait. If he persisted in this deed, perhaps Mr. Pix might hear the story, and Mr. Mere liked to be thought well of by the stewards of the Great.

But who was it that laughed? Mere believed himself to be the man to silence any impertinent watcher.

He opened the window and looked out into the lane. Someone was walking up and down in the still beauty of the summer's night. This man walked a little way, turned, and came back again. He stood and nodded at Mere. He was John Death.

John's hints and admonitions are often most pleasantly presented, with a certain half-grim delight in the innuendo. 'I now mean to enjoy myself in Dodder,' he tells Mr. Hayhoe at their first meeting, the latter having failed to discover his identity:

'I am sure that you will,' said Mr. Hayhoe happily, 'and before you have been a month with us we shall have you baptized, confirmed, and married.'

'But not buried, I hope,' replied Death, smiling.

Throughout the story John shows himself subject to touches of anger, wounded vanity, light malice, envy. When he is annoyed he is likely to derive a compensatory pleasure from some equivocal threat; as here (where the two pennies are of course those which are placed on the eyes in death):

'You promised me a penny when you went away,' said Winnie.

'And I will give you two pennies, when we meet again,' replied Death grimly.

He is delighted to look upon the 'sleek black coats' of the rooks as they feed upon Joseph Bridle's new-sown barley; he is amused when he sees a hedgehog curl itself up:

He had often, he said, seen people straighten out when he came to them, but never before had he seen a creature turn into a ball.

His love affairs are matters of both self-gratification and

kindness. Sarah Bridle, an imbecile from a girl through the repressive cruelty of her envious mother and the sadistic jocularity of the youthful Mere—she imagines she is a camel—is embraced in love by John and (ultimately) cured. He is usually light-hearted and wanton in his loving. Mr. Solly and Joe Bridle hear low sounds of delight from the parlour sofa; after waiting a short while they enter the house:

> Inside the parlour they found Sarah, resting contentedly upon the sofa, and smoothing her skirts. John Death was sitting next to her, with his arm round her, and was asking her to take him to Baghdad. He informed her, proudly, that he believed that General Gordon was not the only one who could ride a camel.
>
> Death was in the highest spirits, and Sarah looked at him lovingly. Mr. Solly shook hands with them both in high glee.   He called Death 'doctor'.
>
> 'My dear doctor,' he said, your treatment has been excellent; no king's physician could have acted with more propriety. You doctors are knowing fellows. But perhaps you have been in practice for some while.'
>
> 'Only with Daisy Huddy,' replied John, a little disappointedly.

On another occasion, warmth, wantonness, casual-seeming seriousness, and humour give a rich flavour; Mr. Hayhoe has nervously come to Daisy Huddy's cottage with the intention of reforming her by reading Jane Austen to her; he has *Pride and Prejudice* in his pocket; he cannot help feeling relieved when he sees John Death in the room:

> . . . She showed Mr. Hayhoe a golden bangle, of very old and curious workmanship. Mr. Hayhoe looked at Death, mournfully.
>
> 'Of course she would not take it for nothing,' said John gaily.
>
> 'Oh, but that was nothing,' laughed Daisy. 'And I never knew I could get so much given to me—I mean

so pretty a thing—for doing so little, and I pleased John so well, that he said my body was like a dove's breast.'

Mr. Hayhoe looked out of the window.

'It was only kind to show Daisy,' observed Death, 'that there are happier usages in love's doings than that damned Farmer Mere has ever shown to her.'

'How do you know that Farmer Mere is damned?' enquired Mr. Hayhoe.

'I met some one walking on Madder Hill who told me so,' replied Death.

'Perhaps you mean Tinker Jar,' said Mr. Hayhoe. Death nodded.

'I have come to make Daisy happy, too,' cried Mr. Hayhoe. Death bowed. He went to the stairway door, that he opened widely. Mr. Hayhoe turned very red.

'Oh!' he cried, 'you mistake my meaning, John. I only meant that I would make Daisy happy by reading a book to her.'

'Ah!' said Death. 'If that is so, then I will certainly stay and listen, for I believe that you have Keats' Odes in your pocket. He's a fine poet and knows whom to praise when he listens in a darkening evening to the song of a nightingale. And now, after Daisy and I have been so happy in one another's company, to hear a good poem read will give us both pleasure.'

John's successes are with Sarah and Daisy; he fails in his designs on Winnie and Priscilla. His profoundest love is for Susie Dawe, as hers is for him; it is not consummated. Allegorically, however, she becomes Death's when she (having been raped by Mere) and Joe drown themselves in the pond. Rising out of that 'allegorically' it can be said at this point that to my mind *Unclay* is to some degree impaired by a certain confusion of intention, manifesting itself mainly in the *human* nature of John Death, in the nature of his love, which is sometimes love as we normally understand it and sometimes a desire to bring to death, to possess in death. Hence his love is exercised sometimes with benefit to the living and sometimes it simply signifies their bodily destruction. Further confusion comes from the simultaneous view of death as both retribution and a state of peaceful content. If *Unclay* were wholly comedy these things wouldn't matter at all; as it is they reveal what seems like some uncertainty of attitude in Powys. The John Death who cures Sarah, who shows Daisy that even lust can solace and be kind, is also the John Death who with witty gruesome *doubles ententres* exults in his real vocation of bringer of death to the suffering:

'I know a great deal about women, more than you think I do, Mr. Mere. I have been the first with a number of them. They lie in bed and call to me to come to them. Of course I tantalise them a little. One cannot always be potent in an instant when one is wanted.   A man so much in request as I has to hold back sometimes. Ah! you think that you alone can make a young maid cry out, but I do so too, when I come to them. I give them pains for their pennies. Their tortured bodies cry and groan and drip blood because of my sweet embraces.

'When I approach these fair ones—and I always appear stark naked—their young eyes grow dim, and droop in their excess of love. When I come to a girl she does not know her own mother. As soon as I enter the bedroom, the pretty things will often cast off all their clothing and lie naked before me. They lie in agony because of my love.'

There is however an important factor which resolves in many places in *Unclay* the seemingly contradictory attitudes: this is the view of love as a destroyer of peace, a mine, an abyss. If we accept this, and remember also his claim to be a bringer of peace, we shall understand John's words to Priscilla:

'Here is your child's grave. I kill, and Love gives life, but in reality we are one and the same. We often exchange our weapons. And then 'tis I that give life, and Love that kills.'

Over and over again we have explicit affirmations of this view
of love:

> As soon as love fastened the burden upon Joe, the
> peace of Madder Hill left him . . . The thought of
> Susie filled him utterly; she was the universe, she was
> a terrible monster, and yet the sweetest thing that ever
> man saw.

We are told that 'Love never pities. He mocks all and destroys
many.' Here is Susie:

> And because she was tormented, she wished to
> torment. Her own body rebelled and bit her; let her
> bite another! Her girlhood was now become something
> dangerous, something that wished to harm.
>
> She knew what she must do; to pain in a subtle
> manner is easy to a woman. To lie down where the
> yellow flowers grow, to show a woman's cunning
> intimacy, nearer and yet a little nearer guiding the
> steps of her victim, who sees no further than her allure-
> ments, until straightway he falls into the abyss.

And here are the ways of the 'common man' and the 'fine
gentleman':

> Cunningly to devise mischief, to bite the life out of
> her heart, to drive a poor creature into madness, to
> cast down a girl and to pour upon her the issue
> of many a foul desire, that is the way of a common
> man. To plume himself, to strut like a barncock, to
> tease and torment his prey, that is the way of a fine
> gentleman.

Instances could be multiplied, and if they represented the
whole tone of *Unclay* we should have to speak of something
like a sombre bitterness. Of course they do not.

But there are more 'cynicisms' and 'horrors' that have to
be glanced at in an endeavour to reconcile them with a total
view of the book which would justify, at least in some measure,
a dictum from *Unclay* itself: 'In every good book a light shines,
that compels the reader to be joyful'. The sense of life's having

in store pitfall after pitfall is strong in *Unclay*, and at the same
time death is but an equivocal blessing:

Then beware, it is best to let sleeping gods alone.
The mortal who arouses a god out of his slumber must
be prepared for any conceivable calamity. He had
better at once cover his head with ashes and his loins
with sackcloth. A god may stir generously, he may open
his hand, and stretch out his arm to give a good gift—
and what gift, God-a-mercy, will that be? A grave.

Destruction and terror may come at any moment:

She liked to see how they jumped and tumbled, and
fancied they were entirely happy in their games. No
one hindered or rebuked them, no dog barked, no
fox was abroad. Near to the warren there was a
stunted elder-bush that had withstood many a
winter's storm, and was now garmented with scented
flowers. The rabbits played about this bush in high
glee. There was nothing to disturb their enjoyment;
they could leap and be merry. When they wanted
to rest, they nibbled the sweet grass.

But suddenly and quite unexpectedly a large black
rabbit seized a young doe. The doe screamed. A
magpie called out 'Murder!' and every rabbit scam-
pered in a hurry to his burrow.

The hillside was now entirely deserted; there
was not a creature to be seen. The warren might have
been uninhabited, and the elder-tree might have
lived there for ever alone.

Your trust in God will avail you nothing:

There is a certain name that is best left alone . . .
A man is wise who lives to himself alone, and forgets
that Name.

If this Name, by some unlucky chance, is hidden
in thy heart, cast it out. Away with it, away with it!
It is a torment, a terrible fang . . . Take it into the
church, and carry yourself along too, in the robes of

a bishop, place the Name upon the Altar, and the old
serpent will devour it. Then power, praise and might,
goods and honour will come to you; with that Name
out of your sight, you will be rich.

Akin, even though distantly, to the apprehension or bitterness
revealed in these recognitions, are the several descriptions of
the physically loathsome. ('Corruption' is a common word in
*Unclay*.) The two most prominent occur in the chapters, 'The
Name', and 'The Best Liquor'. They are not merely descriptions, of course; they are situation and narrative too, with a
certain ominous note and a moral significance. When Joe
Bridle finds John Death's parchment—

*UNCLAY*
*Susie Dawe*
*Joseph Bridle—*

floating on the pond in his field, and gathers it, to the
accompaniment of disorders in the sky and the trees and the
animal world, various creatures and things appear from the
water and in one way or another assail him and strive to wrest
it from him: swarming newts and vipers, corpses with dripping
fingers, a lovely inviting nymph, a beautiful boy, a slimy
stinking toad, a mass of decayed carrion rising from the
bottom of the pond, a snake crawling from a child's body, are
items in an account which, while it is much more than a
catalogue of horrors—Joe's firmness in love is stressed; at the
same time there is a hint of the troubles ahead for him—and
though it is cool and exact in manner, is more impressionistic
and sensational than powerfully significant. It is unusual, it
has various points of interest that make it more than simple
melodrama, but it has not the rich dramatic economy of (say)
the *Mr. Weston* chapter, 'Mr. Grunter Finds his Lost Boot'.
The mere repulsiveness is too clamorous. We have much the
same feeling from 'The Best Liquor', in which the men in the
Bullman Arms, their drink paid for by John Death (with
Roman coins which he has rifled from his only source of
income—tombs), drink their fill and see one another as

cadavers within the strange darkness that fills the parlour: a worm crawls from Mr. Mere's rotting eye, Dady is a corpse wherein the flies he has killed are breeding maggots, Dillar's jaw is fallen and stiff, and so on. In this chapter, as in 'The Name', there are things which are not at all purveyances of horror, but the details of this particular part of it—blackened gums, 'moving in a ghastly manner', mouldy hands—seem unnecessarily insistent for the *memento mori* purpose they serve. Powys is deliberate in all this, of course; the writing is controlled, there is no nervous excitement. But the note of the corruption and the stench of *Unclay* is like that of the asseverations of the disastrous nature of love, in the suggestion it gives of the writer forcing his thought and material in his determination to present truths in contradistinction to conventional and popular idealisations.

The general propositions about love in *Unclay* are not deduced from the representatives of love in the action. Powys isn't naïvely offering a set of poor lovers and then saying 'Look, that's what love is'. The propositions are firmly expressed, they stand in their own right, they have much interest and considerable plausibility. But one can imagine an *Unclay* which would have been more compelling with lovers of greater character, greater intelligence. Joe Bridle is heavily persistent, faithful, but too slow and stupid for Susie; Mere is cruel lust only; Daisy Huddy is a kind, colourless harlot; Mr. Solly is inexperienced and frightened of love, and his association with the girl Winnie, though portrayed with wit and tenderness, is no more than fancifully symbolical; Hayhoe and Priscilla are meek, gently sorrowful and resigned; the union of Mr. Balliboy and the cured imbecile Sarah is no more than mentioned. John Death, kind and pleasantly wanton, is the best of them, but of course he is the most equivocal of lovers. In *Unclay* there is no inevitability of connection between the many given explicit statements and the action; and though with repeated readings the novel is clearly seen to be less episodic than at first it appears to be (with its fifty-odd chapters to three hundred and forty pages) it does lack organic structure of the profoundest kind, and this entails a loss in force.

But no account of *Unclay* should end on a negative note. Both its material and its tone show that Powys was as seriously engaged as anywhere else in his work. Many of the incidents and situations are in themselves impressive: the meeting of Mr. Hayhoe and John Death; the miser Dawe offering his daughter to the brutal Mere; the chapter called 'A Debt Paid', in which Mere, after passing (with John) Tinker Jar and listening to the words of a funeral service, pays to John the money he owes him; these and others have the Powysian quality that is imparted by the combination of vivid original narrative and moral weight with ironic-humorous touches in the dialogue. Unpleasant truths about human beings frequently appear with a convincing terseness:

> Mr. Dady believed in art—the art of killing. He liked to kill slowly. He would approach a fly, with his thumb going nearer and yet nearer, and the fly supposed that all was well. Then Mr. Dady would squeeze the insect against the pane.

> *Of Mere:* To hurt was his pleasure, it was an act that he liked. He liked to see a creature in torment.

> Mr. Dawe examined the market. He looked out for a buyer. Having a girl to part with, Mr. Dawe became all at once interested in the behaviour of men. He regretted that all men were not chaste. If men were allowed to misbehave with women, then Susie's price would be lowered. With women common, a girl would go cheap. James Dawe hated a harlot.

> *Of Mere and Dawe plotting together:* In every gesture of Mr. Mere's, there was the certainty that he could never be over-reached. Each word of James Dawe's was as subtle as a serpent's glide. Greed drew near to Cunning, and Mischief winked.

But John Death's geniality and wit are a value of the novel too, and Mr. Solly often speaks good sense: whatever the follies and turmoil of human life he knows that 'Madder Hill is the same yesterday, to-day, and for ever'; and it is Mr. Solly who

> had often observed that cool, still water is the best sanctifier of human thought, and that to look for only a few moments into a deep pond, must calm and ease all those wayward flutterings of a man's folly, and give to him instead the holy and blessed thought of an everlasting peace.

The theme, however, of the union of Mr. Solly and Winnie seems overplayed: the nut trees he has planted to keep love out appear rather too often. And Winnie, with all her gay challenges to Death and the 'charming' impudence of her remarks, including her quotations from Jane Austen, appears as only a very light humorous positive. As does Lord Bullman, relenting from his purpose to exercise the 'droit de seigneur' over the bride, Susie.

I see *Unclay* as an extremely interesting and challenging novel, imperfect in ways that are sometimes more obvious than we feel they ought to be in a writer of Powys's stature, and yet with qualities enough not only to justify his own dictum, already quoted, 'In every good book a light shines, that compels the reader to be joyful', but also to serve as an illustration for Lawrence's: 'In every great novel, who is the hero all the time? Not any of the characters, but some unnamed and nameless flame behind them all'. I would not quite call *Unclay* a great novel, but the character and sensibility it reveals would justify us in speaking of the pre-eminence of 'some unnamed and nameless flame', even though in one sense it has undeniably for hero, John Death.

*Chapter Six*

# STYLE AND LANGUAGE

To THINK at random of a dozen English writers in connection
with their styles is to conclude that the usefulness of such
thinking varies immensely with the writers. At one end of the
scale are mannerisms that can be listed and deductions that
can be made from the repetition of devices; at the other there
is writing where discussion of style becomes discussion of a
sensibility and a whole technique. A distinctive style, in the
sense of being recognisable as peculiar to one author, does not
necessarily mean significant writing; often the contrary. If
after showing early promise a writer does not grow in response
and understanding, he may well end up with a 'distinctive'
bag of tricks. It would be true to say that the more considerable
the writer the more his initial idiosyncrasies are absorbed into
a style which, though still his, is remarkable more for its total
impact than for detachable personal devices.

In making the generalisation that the writings of T. F.
Powys (with the possible exception of his first book, the
*Interpretation of Genesis*) are marked by an original style, the
sort of originality that is meant is not one that is striking merely
by virtue of novelty. Although it is possible to isolate certain
qualities of that originality, T. F. Powys's writing is one of those

cases where style and substance are in the last analysis inseparable.

If diction were the main criterion, there would not be a
simpler writer in the language than T. F. Powys. He is content
with the words of everyday use, and he never gives them
arbitrary meanings. Likewise there are no inversions or
convolutions of language. Yet his use of the ordinary yields a
style which gives us as a main impression the sense of successful
endeavour to write as if from scratch, starting again with a new
and fresh and simple language to convey a new and fresh
vision of things and happenings and people.

The style of Powys's second book, *Soliloquies of a Hermit,*
differs sharply from that of *An Interpretation of Genesis,* and in it
can be seen the beginnings of the individual style which
appeared in *The Left Leg* and which was sustained, with
enriching modifications in certain works and with slackening
of tension in others, to the end of his writing life. The *Genesis,*
which is in the form of a dialogue between Moses the Lawgiver
and Zetetes the Seeker (who is Powys), and which encompasses
discussion of man's nature, man and woman and sex, the birth
of moral consciousness, self-regard, the growth of possessiveness,
death and so on, is for the most part self-consciously archaic in
style. It incorporates a lot of Biblical language as well as often
being palpably Biblical in its phrases and cadences. Where it is
simple the simplicity tends to be affected, and its obscurities
are due largely to an orotund manner. The searching for 'truth'
is genuine in its concern and the thought is often interesting
(without being compelling), but the book has a very limited
intrinsic value. Its general style may be indicated by this:

> Thou hast climbed up to the height whereon I stand;
> dost thou expect to find here the same lilies that grow
> in the valley? In the valley are the flowers and the
> soft winds; if thou desire them return unto them; leave
> me upon my height amongst the desolate and great
> rocks, leave me, I say, and return again to the Mother
> in the valley.

The great advance in stylistic power that we see in *Soliloquies of a Hermit* corresponds to a greater personal urgency in Powys's approach. The *Soliloquies* is as much a 'search' as the *Genesis*, but despite the unusual opening it is much more a matter of day-to-day living, and in being more intimate it works at a deeper level of sincerity than the studied eloquence of the *Genesis* will allow. Compare this for example with the lines just quoted:

> I try to deepen, to broaden, to open my life in every
> way; to stand no more wondering how to be happy,
> but to see and feel and touch. I like to touch the waves
> of the sea and the mould in my garden; I like to touch
> the heart of man; I like to touch the grass and moss of
> the fields.

And when eloquence occurs in the *Soliloquies*, the personal note is not obliterated and Powys remains lucid, as when expressing resentment at invasion by the modern 'devil':

> There is something in the spirit of these modern days
> that makes me feel that I am wasting time when I am
> reading, and that 'something' must be the iron-eyed,
> restless, nail-making devil that tries to put petrol into
> every man's belly, and would turn the world into a
> scurvy heap of scurrying ants, all running every way
> inside large white eggs that move themselves, a great
> many times bigger than the little ants. And even I that
> live in the wilderness, sitting in my own hut between
> the hills that are now covered with yellow gorse
> flowers—even I, with brown bread and tea upon the
> table, and my feet to the fire—even I, sitting thus in
> the desert, feel the devil tugging at my coat and
> shouting in my ear that I ought to be doing something
> in order to help the nail-makers to iron over the whole
> world. It is terrible to think that the evil smell of
> modern oil has got to me, and that the vile working
> devils would even try to pump petrol into my soul.
> In heaven's name let those that make work into a god

H

with a Brummagem name, take him out of my way; I
do not like that kind of god.

A simple epigrammatic balance characterises the style in many
places of the *Soliloquies* :

The fact that it is hard to get anything out of oneself
drives people to go and get what they can out of others.

Sometimes he works with seeming paradox, as in 'immortal'
below, and with the irony of under-statement:

A gentleman came here once for the shooting; he
came from town. I may as well say here that he
belonged to the immortal type of man; and when he
was not shooting he attached himself to me, and he
found me very ready to listen to his *bons mots*, although
they were not quite in the same style as our Saviour's.

When the explicit searching and the pondering of these two
works become the artistic statements that the novels and
short stories manifestly are, the language takes on new qualities
of surprise and vividness.

Ironic effects of the more simple kind, simple though
amusing and often quite sharp in impact, occur everywhere:

'Dear children'—that was the way the Bishop had
begun his address. The dear children loafed out on to
the heath, killing, on their way, a thrush and a hedge-
sparrow. The earth that had brought them forth
remained pensive about them. (*Mr. Tasker's Gods*).

Incompatible viewpoints may be tellingly suggested:

Mr. Tarr looked at Mr. Pink, and decided that he
would be happy as a Methodist preacher.

'The country people are ignorant here,' he remarked forcefully; 'they are low in the scale of being;
they are like underdone mutton, they want to be
baked by salvation, they're all bloody.'

'I fear they're not always as kind to one another
as they should be,' said Mr. Pink; 'and as I am Mr.
Roddy's representative, I am forced to hear a great
deal that I am sorry for.'

'The people want salvation,' said Mr. Tarr.

'They want kindness,' said Mr. Pink.

The sort of mild terseness shown in that passage from *Mockery Gap* takes on a sharper edge when an unsympathetic character is being delineated. In this general portrait of a miser the words cut sharply and shrewdly into the very character of the type:

> He believes in unity; if he holds one penny in his hand, it is all that he thinks he has. He hoards only units. He believes that his belly is a bank, and his guts hiding-places for gold. What passes from him, he regards as lost. His most constant fear is that his store may go into the belly of another. When he has lent anything, he would like to rip up his neighbour's body and find his gold again. . . .
>
> Where another would see nothing, he sees a great deal. A little coal dust in a shed, a despised heap of small sticks—these he sees as a fine estate. Nothing escapes his wary eye. He will not pass by the smallest nail or piece of string. What other people throw away, he could live upon. He lives by adding one to one. He is a fine leveller.
>
> He goes from one sale to another. He buys at one, a great house; at another, a rotten mattress. He sees these two purchases as the same, but the mattress pleases him the best. A bug in it is a good omen; when he rips up the mattress, he finds money . . .
>
> (*Unclay*).

Here the dry force and succinctness of the manner come from his understanding of the miser's mentality and from an interest which is not motivated by distaste alone. The aptness of the objects chosen for their relevance to the miser's life strengthens the impression of hard exactness.

Although this kind of selection of richly suggestive objects is not primarily a matter of style, it is closely connected with it and it is pervasive in Powys; the objects however small have a

certain symbolic effectiveness. The genteel Miss Pettifer in
*Innocent Birds* is associated with a horror of margarine, which is
reserved for the servant. When Maud has brought by mistake
margarine instead of butter into the rectory drawing-room,
Miss Pettifer eats her tea in quick short bites, crunching up the
little stones in the cake; she then begins to knit angrily:

> The needles clicked sharply, and Miss Pettifer gazed at
> the lilac blossom that bloomed prettily on the chair
> covers. The chair covers were certainly saying as she
> was—that Maud must go.

Odd turns of fancy produce unexpected collocations:

> Mrs. Crocker had taught Solly to fear two important
> things in this world. God was one of them, damp
> clothes was the other. (*Innocent Birds*).

An unusual simile may be used to lower the value of the object
it is illuminating:

> Her hands sprawled upon the table with the wine-
> glass between them like two dead fish that had been
> cast ashore. These fish had chapped red backs and dull
> dirty-white bellies. (*Mark Only*).

or to raise the value of the object by comparing it with something which in normal valuation exists on a higher plane of
existence:

> A good kitchen is a home fit for the blessed saints,
> where all is warmth, comfort, and good victuals, and
> where two great warming-pans shine ever upon the
> walls like the cheeks of God. (*Kindness in a Corner*).

The geniality here enfolds warming-pans, saints, and God.
Occasionally there is a more complicated image, as in this
from *Innocent Birds:*

> Modesty, that careful sentiment, placed as a sun-dew
> in a maiden's heart to catch brides—after their human
> blood is sucked dry—for heaven, now left Maud
> defenceless.

When we know that the leaves of the beautifully named plant
entrap and absorb insects, a certain horror accompanies the

lightly cynical description of modesty as 'a careful sentiment', and this effect reinforces the playing-off of the spiritualised maiden and brides and heaven against that stark cynicism in parenthesis.

Effective stylisation of the Dorset dialect is a feature of many of Powys's stories. In the earthy-local atmosphere of *Mark Only*, Mark's speeches are sometimes given a rhythm which helps to emphasise the pathos of his case—stupid as he is, and nearly blind, and bewildered by life—and to lend him a kind of human dignity in his hopeless apartness. Here is part of his long soliloquy as he sits, on the night of his wedding, on the low wall near the village green:

'Church bain't a good place to be in,' he muttered,
' 'tis a place where folk do look, and where noises do
look. Every one did stare at I an' I did hear something.
'Twas only they dogs' feet a-pattering. Mrs. Maggs
were staring at I, and I did think—they dogs be shut up
in church tower. Parson Hayball 'ave shut up tower
door so that dogs shouldn't get out at I. But I did
listen while folk did stare.

'Up and down tower steps they did scamper, same
as I heared they about in lane when father died. I did
thinkie up by golden rails, when parson were talking,
"Who be they after now with their red tongues
hanging out, bain't I, be it, bain't I?" . . .

'What be I looking for in evening darkness; be it
stable, or be it they hills? Nell were the one to take
a chap away from they high hills, she 'ave draw'd I
down away from blowing winds, she 'ave draw'd I
down to where they dogs do patter and go.'

The method there, with the soliloquy convention and the heightened rhythm of the dialect, is comparatively simple, and so is the communicated feeling. For something more quietly subtle we may look at a passage from that fine startling allegory, *The Two Thieves*. After the long relentless exposure of George Douse's vileness, his way of life having been reflected through a cool hardness of style with many ironies and curt savageries, there comes the moment in the story when the second thief, Tinker Jar (Christ), visits the dying John Roe, to take from him, if he has them about him, Anger, Greed, Pride, and Cruelty:

'I have a reason for the theft,' replied Jar, 'because such sins are a burden that I alone must bear. Yield them to me.'

The thief searched, with a deep look, the soul of John Roe.

'And have you no anger, then,' he said at length, 'against George Douse?'

'Was it my doing,' replied John Roe, 'that George Douse was born into the world to steal away Alice from me? Who can commit a greater folly than to be angry with God?'

The thief blushed and looked away.

'I think you have a little pride left,' he said. 'You are proud of dying so fearlessly in the company of a thief.'

'I have examples for doing so, and only copy others,' replied John Roe, 'and as I am in no pain at the moment, though I breathe with difficulty, I am hopeful that Nature will rid me of this life as naturally and no more unkindly than she brought me into being.'

'Ah! but you wish to be cruel to yourself,' cried the thief. 'You wish to blame and torment yourself for your misdeeds. You sorrow for your miserable days, and you desire to raise up the everlasting terror of hell in your mind, so that you may die fearfully.'

'On the contrary,' replied John Roe, 'I wish to treat myself with the greatest gentleness, and I hope that Nature will be gentle too. I am tired, and I look soon to be at peace for ever.'

'But your greed?' said the other. 'You yourself have

shown me that you still hoard. You have even kept ten pounds in your drawer until this very day.'

'I did not wish it to be said,' replied John Roe, with a smile, 'by the householders of Godsbarrow that it was all through the burying of my poor carcass that the rates rose so high.'

Tinker Jar regarded John Roe yet more lovingly.

'I see then,' he said, 'that I have come where nothing can be stolen, but can you not tell me of one, richer in these goods than yourself, whom I may rob of them?'

'You will not learn that from me,' replied John Roe.

'I will go and find what I seek myself, then,' said the thief, 'but you will not be left long alone, for I think that I hear the step of another visitor coming this way.'

'I am ready,' said John Roe.

The thief softly opened the door. And, as he did so, the winds that had but a little before blown less boisterously were quite stilled, and the moon shone very clear.

John Roe turned his face to the window.

The thief stood for a moment in the doorway, as though to admit some one, and while he stood there, though no wind blew, yet the candle upon the table went out . . .

The flexible rhythms of the vernacular, in their quieter aspect, suggest the movements of mind and feeling inherent in the situation, especially the acceptance and assurance of John Roe.

Quiet assurance is commoner in Powys than fervour, but lyrical passages do occur, as when the glow-worm (in *John Told and the Worm*), lying in Farmer Told's hand, makes its appeal to his sense of beauty:

' . . . It's a pleasant thing to hold an enemy in one's grasp, and as soon as I am rested I will place you in the path, and the light you boast of will guide my boot so that I can trample you to death.'

When she heard this sentence pronounced upon her, the glow-worm remained pensive for a while, but even then she did not lose heart nor did she despair of escaping, though she remained in the farmer's hand.

'Have you never thought, Squire Told,' she began gently, 'that, even if we exempt virtue and goodness, there are in the world other pleasant things more delightful than a mere possession of goods? Is there not the exquisite joy that beauty yields to its votaries, for who would wish his thought, upon such a night as this, to be occupied with the price of pork, with the manuring of a turnip field, or the killing of a little worm? How much better to contemplate the divine loveliness of the summer stars! Look upward and behold the glittering heavens! Does not such a sight awake in your mind a state of blessedness? Notice, too, I pray you, that heavy mass of blackness that is Madder Hill; see how it is set against the midnight sky. Does not the profound darkness of the hill suit the mild and deep melancholy that can join the Creator to the creature in one large sorrow? Hark you, listen to that distant sound, that heavy fall of the sea upon the summer beach! Think of the cool shining of the pebbles and the white loneliness of the great cliffs. Consider the eternal, the everlasting look of the sea itself. Think again, Mr. Told, for a moment, upon a white daytime flower. You should know all love and sorrow when you see a meek daisy—a small plant, but one that can exceed Solomon in all his glory.'

The speech is eloquent with persuasive cadences and quietly dramatic alternations of question and answer, giving the required impression of clever yet sincere argument-pleading. That the appeal fails, and that what succeeds is a call to the farmer's notice of the approaching footsteps of a girl, may modify the persuasiveness of the speech in retrospect but does not affect its intrinsic beauty.

A neat and easy skill in quoting or referring to other writers is a feature in Powys which though not usually of central importance is sometimes an essential part of a whole effect. Felicitous too are many of the names he gives to people and places: Tommy Toole, Mr. Bugby, Miss Pettifer, Lord Bullman, Mrs. Tite, Minnie Cuddy, Charlie Tulk and many others have in their context an amusing or slightly sinister aptness. Lots of his names however have no specific flavour: Norbury and Shelton are common as actual village names; the curiously named Tadnol is a tiny hamlet on Winfrith Heath. Folly Down is of course self-explanatory—'Lord, what fools these mortals be!' There is a village near Mappowder called Folly. Dodderdown and Dodder take on a little additional interest when we know that dodder is a small parasitic plant known in Dorset; madder is the name of a flower as well as an epithet, and particularly Powysian are his villages of Madder and God's Madder ('God's a queer fellow,' we read in *The Left Leg*). Powys never explains the origins of the names, and when we find out about them we feel the touch of humour in their creation. It is not likely however that anyone will claim for the names anything more than a lightly quaint significance.

Perhaps the central impression left by Powys's style is that of everyday language being controlled to a rich economy, and refined without loss of firmness and solidity. The same could be said, of course, for much distinguished writing. But I cannot think of anyone, even the author of *Huckleberry Finn* (so utterly different from Powys in many ways), who excels him in his mastery of the simple style that expresses the complex man. Other parts of the present book help to demonstrate how Powys's style is the outcome of much thought, much reading, and above all an attitude to life. He found man's moral life a theme for amusement as well as compassion, but his mockery was not frivolity; and the fascination that he found in the forms of everyday life did not turn him into a superior spectator. A church in Powys is always a country church with its quiet architectural beauty and the feeling it gives of what the centuries have left there; and at the unfrequented back of the church are a heap of sweet grass-cuttings, a rusty wheel-barrow, and a lean-to shed with a few tools and an ash-bin. It is because human living, around us now and always, is never forgotten by Powys, that his style is unique in its combination of homeliness and strength.

*Chapter Seven*

## BELIEFS AND IDEAS

THE LACK of momentous outward happenings in the life of T. F. Powys is perhaps proportionate to the fullness of his contemplative self. Immediately it must be said that his contemplation was not that of the withdrawn introspective thinker: one of the main impressions given by his writings is that of a remarkably consistent interest in the day-to-day details of living, in home and village. His pondered conclusions came primarily out of his own observation, his own feelings; that this was so does not mean that he did not put his reading, which was extensive, to the best use. Clearly, the widening offered by reading can also confirm and modify native tendencies and strengthen growth.

In addition to this central and unseen growth, it is possible to point to innumerable places in Powys and remark, 'That sentiment recalls Freud; that is like Nietzsche; that is Lao-Tse'. Powys is fond of generalising in his stories; a small volume of abstracted 'thoughts' could be compiled. But in all his best work it is done with an easy artistic tact which obviates any suggestion of sententiousness or dogmatism. The generalisations are not tacked-on interests; they are integral. And it is only in the fullness, the totality of the creative work, the story, that the 'ideas' are to be appreciated in their plausibility or their force. The stories are marked by a moral vividness or complexity which tells much more than even the weightiest axiom.

Nevertheless, and the more particularly in the case of writers whose works aren't always easily accessible, I believe a little time may be usefully spent in looking at some of their explicitly given ideas and sentiments. It does not matter, at this point, how impressive, or how witty, or how raw, or how trite, the expression of them may be. Our concern is with the nature of the material of the pondering and with the offered opinions: not as final truths—profound as many of them are and ultimate as many of them seem—but as significant interests of an original literary artist. These can be presented here with a minimum of comment.

'God' is always near the surface of Powys's consciousness. More than once he has been described as a seeker after God. This is true as far as it goes, but the search for God, in Powys, means primarily search for the truth about the nature of life and man's place and destiny in the universe. It has nothing to do with dogma or with righteousness. 'I am without a belief,' he says in *Soliloquies of a Hermit*, 'a belief is too easy a road to God'.

Mr. Jar is often a form of God in a Powys story; Mr. Weston is a form of God. But if one had to give as inclusive an indication as possible of what God is, in Powys, a passage like the following might be chosen:

> Grave mould was not plain mould to Gillet now. He saw all Madder afire with the Spirit. Life and death, the creatures, even ants under a stone all burning. The queer presence within had opened his eyes. He saw every blade of grass, every leaf, every movement of the wind, every little red worm, as possessed of God. God shone in the light of the glow-worm that crawled upon the dry slopes of the little hills. He danced lively in the shining eyes of the lizard. He moved with the maggots in the dew-wet

carcass of a rabbit, that had died of fright—fright of
Him. His fancy reached men. He was the coloured
outer ring of Mad Button's mind. He tickled naughty
Nellie till she blamed the fleas. The slow tread of
Eli Squibb going home to dinner, the footed sound
was His. The soft longings of Mrs. Cuddy—?

No; we must not let Him stray so far; His own
Church might read Him a lesson. (*The Left Leg*).

God is the creator of everything, He is in everything. A
profound God-consciousness has always been:

> And then as the light of day wanes and the darkness
> gathers, and we behold the far reaches of the deep,
> we are led to contemplate the grand vista of eternity.
> Then the dark waters gather tumultuously about the
> golden gate of the grave, behind which stands the
> Name, spoken with holy dread by all generations
> of mankind.
>
> Spoken with awe unfathomable. For whatever we
> may think of the injustice, the cruelty, the pain here
> upon earth, the Name, and the terror and love of it
> that hides so silent behind the tomb, must for ever
> hide, too, the ultimate truth. God, for ever and ever-
> lasting, life without end—God. (*Mockery Gap*).

He is all-powerful. When Joe Bridle read the signature on the
parchment which gave the order to 'unclay' Susie and himself,
and had turned his eyes away, he had seen

> Something that in the same moment could Unclay a
> man, let a star fade into nothingness, turn a city into
> a wilderness, and create a fair garden of life in empty
> space. A name that could hurl a sun across the firma-
> ment and make an emmet hurry across a lane upon
> Shelton Heath. (*Unclay*).

He is the implacable author of evil and of good:

> Sometimes at dawn the awful will of the Almighty
> rises to do good, and sets—when the evening comes
> —to do evil. There is no holding back His terrible

purpose. In His right hand He holds evil, in His left good; He deals out as He chooses. Man can do nothing. God is no tamed beast. (*Unclay*).

Men may distinguish and separate good from evil, but they are finally victims like everything else:

> In every sack of seed that comes from the great storehouse, there is a mixture of good corn and bad. Only a white dove can tell the difference, and that dove is always being caught and killed by an old cat—God. (*Unclay*).

But though God has such awful power, He does manifest Himself in humble and familiar form. When Priscilla in *Unclay* asks John Death if his master comes to Dodder, and if so, what is he dressed in,

> 'His only garment is a thunder-cloud,' John replied—'but he sometimes mends kettles . . . '

God preserves as well as destroys:

> ''Ave 'ee ever seen a dead man?' asked Tolly suddenly, though in a true earthy tone.
>
> 'I've seen the drowned boot of woon,' replied Peach. ''Twas when I went down to river for a bundle of they soaked spars, an' the foot of poor Tom were sticking up out of water. " 'Tisn't for Mike Peach to disturb God's doings," I did say, so I did let they spars bide.'
>
> 'You don't thinkie,' inquired Tolly, 'that God 'Isself did pitch poor silly Tom into thik river, for if 'E be so playful, 'tis most like 'E did take and throw wold Peter off ladder.'
>
> ' 'Tis when I be up thatching farmer's high barn that I do think most of wold God's manners,' said Mr. Peach, 'an' I do think that if 'E were minded to cast I down, 'E'd a-do it wi' a finger-push. But I do mind when ladder be shaky that one day when I did fall from barley-stack, that God did move a girt stone from under en, so I fell on soft straw instead of on thik stone.' (*Mark Only*).

A fundamental Powysian idea is that which relates God to, and sometimes virtually equates Him with, the everlasting instincts and feelings in man and other creatures. This and its kindred and tributary ideas have their fullest explicit statement in *Soliloquies of a Hermit*. The main informing idea of this book is that the emotions and drives and desires of man are the 'moods of God'; men live under their shadow, but they pass quickly through most men, who are ultimately dominated by the 'getting mood'; only the 'priest'—Powys's rather confusing name, in this book, for the poet-thinker type—submits to the full force of the moods, suffers them, often seeks to escape, and tries to understand and calm them. The average man is 'immortal' by virtue of his hard unawareness.

> Man is a collection of atoms through which pass the moods of God—a terrible clay picture, tragic, frail, drunken, but always deep rooted in the earth, always with claws holding on to his life while the moods pass over him and change his face and his life every moment. The people of the earth are clay pieces that the moods of God kindle into life.

The escape from the 'attributes of immortality—greed, hardness of heart, cunning—all the biting instincts of the animal', can be made by approach to Christ. Christ has destroyed that God, who is, in a sense, the God of the Old Testament:

> With the terrible moods of God moving about me, as dark clouds, and then the lightning, and sometimes the ominous silence and calm, I turn to the stranger upon earth that once learned to bear the burden of God, calling Him Father, and holding Him, as Atlas held the world, upon His shoulders.

Christ, representing the antithesis of the 'getting mood', gives value to life:

> It is the spring, and the apple-blossom is beautiful because He is there in it. To love Him is the only good thing in this world. It does not matter if He is

true; He is beyond all Truth. All things have breath in Him; I feel Him in the earth. When I hammer at the rocks and break away fossils that have been there for millions of years, I am only going a little way into His love. When I look up into the night and see the light that has left a star thousands of years ago, I can only see a little way into His love. His love is a terrible love—terrible and deep, hard for a man to bear; I have lived in it, I know it.

But this profound recognition of the spiritual value given to life by Christ's vision and love is not permanently held:

Even now the mood of belief is gone and I turn upon myself and cry out against what I am writing; I shake all the thoughts of love about my ears, and turn Christ into a worm again. I look out again into the mist; I sit and watch the dim evening light that saddens the hills; I see the days pass, the winter days; and I taste the creatures, the bread and the wine; and I do not feel His body in them, the bread and the wine! I feel the emptiness, the unutterable emptiness of all the thoughts in the world; and I hearken to the remote sounds of the sea. I wonder why we can ever leave the simple clearness of our lives, in order to crawl into the underworld of mystery. I see all things common again and myself the commonest of all. I see the Eternal moods casting men over and over again into the same pit, and I see the Christ, a poor dark Arab, lying beaten by the rods of the Roman soldiers, because the wicked sisters of poetry chose him out of all men to teach Truth—Truth that is hateful to men. Christ, like the first swallow, is a promise of summer, but only too well we know that the summer ends, and then comes 'the winter of our discontent'.

Who can blame the men who choose to live the simple life of swagger and bluster and shame?

Sometimes the human life of everyday is the only thing that seems important:

> I look back and see the common things, the human things; not God's moods, or Christ, or the wonder that is called man's soul. I believe that I have shed more tears over my little boy's broken engine that I dug up one day in the garden, than over all the killing of the Son of Man.

There are certain resources of peace, other than Christ, which can sustain against the 'wild moods of God that tear and baffle us'. The Church as it is usually understood was not, for Powys, one of them. Neville's words in *Mr. Tasker's Gods* are in effect his:

> 'The English Church is humanly organized,' he said. 'It has become a very successful business. It took a great work out of loving hands and built in the Master's name a jam factory. They boil the stones of the fruit and call it "Christ's Church".
> —Without Jesus our Church is really splendid.'

What is a source of both consolation and power is the knowledge of an everlasting being and principle of life outside man's orbit:

> But over all that happens, a watcher stands and looks. This watcher is Madder Hill. Above life— that grand and woeful calamity—Madder Hill looks and yields a kind of consolation to those who bend to it. It may be but the sweet odour of white clover, or the winter's sun setting in the sea, that tells other tales than the fury of constant becoming and continuous ending. Madder Hill is the same yesterday, to-day, and for ever. (*Unclay*).

There is the beauty of nature, especially in its quiet manifestations:

> One has only to wink once or twice, and the summer is gone. Gone, with all its yellow gladness that it gave, and gone with all its yellow sadness too.

I

But gone; and so quickly each summer's going is, that we have only to wink the three times, and our lives are gone too, with their early morning sunshine and their long evening shadows.

If so be any happiness has been found by us during our three winks, we have found it—and we all know this to be true—in quiet places. We have met it—if at all—where the fir-cones lie about so kindly that we are almost inclined under those tall and sweet-scented trees to kneel down and worship the earth.

Perhaps upon the warm grassy side of a hill in March, with the cold wind banished behind it, the doors of our soul may have opened for a breath of joy to come in. Or when the bracken first breaks through the soil upon the heath; or when Madder hill, at midnight, makes a black line athwart the stars. If our joy enters not into us at those times, we may bid it farewell for ever. (*Innocent Birds*).

Though melancholy is a frequent companion:

This feeling of melancholy—and Solly even, though he felt it when he looked at his beans in flower, could never say why it was come to him—often grows up with beauty, blossoming when she blossoms, and gives out a deeper sadness than her loveliness can give joy. When we go into the courts of summer—courts of clear colour and fair flowers and sweet scents—a shadow will come by that is best greeted with our tears. This shadow is born with all beauty, and enters into us from the very loveliness that we are beholding, and makes us learn to welcome the rude grosser hours instead of the tantalising moments when beauty stays to sadden us. (*Innocent Birds*).

Colour awakes and enlivens:

It is possible to be awakened from the very saddest state of mind by a sudden burst of colour. A colour that burns can do more than make us merely happy: it can give us life.

The light that lightens the world can shine in a daisy; it can also shine in the human form when it is naked and fair. (*Mockery Gap*).

Sunshine and warmth are celebrated:

Sometimes, the month of November being come— when the almanac gives a picture of a man driving a wedge into a fallen tree, while the rain falls down— Nature, that monstrous and sudden lover, embraces anew the earth with a loving kiss of summer sunshine. The air is clear then, for the October rains have made it so, and the long afternoon shadows, thrown by the great Tadnol elms, please a peaceful mind, while the warm sun—a pretty last blessed gift from an already forgotten summer—gladdens the hearts of those who are wise enough to live in the present moment.

(*Kindness in a Corner*).

To Powys's vision, one of the two great realities—the other is death—is love, human love. About love and lust he has innumerable, and often perplexing and disturbing things to say. Zetetes' archaic language in *An Interpretation of Genesis* expresses a 'Lawrentian' belief:

Thou doest well to take the old story of the poets as to the coming of woman, for woman is in part man and groweth with man, and thine Adam is woman as well as man : and the growing together of the man and the woman hath given to man the key to the Truth, for it is impossible for man to grow alone.

And with this affirmation of love's significance goes an insistence on the difficulties inherent in the very nature of attraction and desire:

A young girl is a deep mystery. When she enters a room something enters with her that belongs to the earth and to the sun, to the carnal and to the holy. A warm, earthy thing, a star of heaven. Pagan and yet

merry with God, a presence that wishes to be kind, but
opens a door to sorrow. (*Kindness in a Corner*).

Nature drives the young women on, they are hounds that
pursue the merry stags; then suddenly they are themselves the
ones that are caught. Sometimes happiness results. But often
their beauty, their sweetness, become a source of suffering
for them, suffering which they seem unable to flee from: the
'god' of love must have his sacrifice:

> . . . And the nearest green bank is used for a
> bridal bed. There, a pretty pastime may be practised
> with sweet usage, or perhaps, instead of loving
> manners, a furious frolic may come of it, cruel and
> hostile to love.
>
> From such doings lust may emanate, or love and
> gentle content.
>
> But perhaps hideous cruelty alone is there, and its
> claws bloody. This wonder may come quick and
> sudden; at other times it is very slow—a ponderous
> bulk that moves to destroy. Or else it shows its
> victim her own face in the glass. It is her own sweetness
> that brought in the terror. She called for the music,
> it was the piper who played. Her outcries, her screams
> are forgotten, and she returns again and again to kiss
> the rod.
>
> Her young eyes, moist and clinging, gaze at the
> terrible sign. Her knees bend tremblingly; she has
> entered the pagan grove where the pole is set up. She
> knows herself to be a sacrifice to the god. The god
> demands her; his prey must be given to him. (*Unclay*).

The coming of love may have a tremendous subversive force:

> But even with these omissions, Joseph Bridle
> succeeded well enough in being merry, until one day.
> That one day comes to all; before then the river of
> life flows smoothly, and all is well.
>
> Then the change comes. The first change—the
> forerunner of Death—is Love. When the sun of Love

rises, and a man walks in its glory, he may be sure
that a shadow approaches him—Death.

Love creates and separates; Death destroys and
heals. A dead thistle-stalk, a fallen ash-leaf are the
same thing. Man, alone, is separate and different from
nature. Love has bewitched, bewildered him. Love
comes up in the dark, and before a man knows what
has happened, he is pricked by an arrow. That stab is
a sign. The man will soon sleep again in an unknowing
consciousness: he will die. He will be like the thistle-
stalk and the dead leaf. Let the young years be long,
there is no trouble in them, let them last: 'Be thou as
little children.'

But to be so is not easy. The day comes, the mine
explodes, the man is blinded, Joe Bridle loves.

(*Unclay*).

The insistence on the immense and universal power of love
in its aspect of an unalloyed 'drive', carries with it the
recognition of a predatory and possessive element. More than
one man in Powys looks at a woman 'as a hawk would at a lark
that sang below him'. More than one woman is fed upon 'as
though she were an extra slice of treacle pudding'.

When Powys generalises on love, the emphasis is usually
on the 'elemental', self-feeding, self-regarding aspect.
Determined at all costs not to flatter, he all too often falls into
imbalance by too frequent references to love as mere
gratification and food for the ego and the body. Agreeing (no
doubt) with Lawrence's feeling of 'All this nonsense about love
and unselfishness, more crude and repugnant than savage
fetish worship', he tended, in his refusal to make any concession
to conventional self-flattering views, to go to the other extreme
and overstress love's underminings and terrors. Sometimes,
however, we get a statement affirming love's power to trans-
form and beautify:

When a young girl feels the hot sap of love rush to
her heart and turn to dance furiously in her veins,

because she knows that the consummation of all her
most secret thought and desires is at hand, she isn't
likely to go quietly to her home to join her father at
supper. She prefers the darkness of the night that
may ease perhaps the agony of her suspense. The
deepest darkness she transforms in a moment, for her
light shines like a glow-worm's, and the night air is
bewitched with wonder. (*Mr. Weston's Good Wine*).

And in the same novel, Luke Bird, addressing the old horse that
is spending its last days in peace and quiet upon the downs, is
clearly speaking for Powys when he asks for a sympathetic
understanding of the almost infinite variety of the actions
prompted by love:

'Only such a modest creature as you,' said Luke,
patting its neck, 'is fit to hear me. I do not know much
about love, but this I do know, that in all its
ramifications, in all its manifold appearances, it should
be used kindly. Love is the only thing in the world;
all else is weariness and wormwood. In its wildest
flights, in its most grotesque attitudes, love remains
untainted. Unhappiness would fade and perish if love
were always kind. All amusements that gather about
this wonderful loadstone should be ever treated by all
the committees of the world with tolerance and
magnanimity. And the most strange abnormalities
of love, its most distorted and fantastical expressions,
should but be viewed by the magistrates as the rage
of God.' (*Mr. Weston's Good Wine*).

Affirmations of the value of interdependence and companion-
ship are sometimes made:

In the country, married joy can still be found. Life
can be merry and happy where keen winter blasts
and the smoke of autumn bonfires keep the devil
away. Two straws, blown into a corner, hold together;
the dark night keeps them near each other. One never
knows when Madder Hill may begin to talk; and

> when fear creeps in under the stairs, two are better
> than one. (*Unclay*).

But despite the presence of passages like these, a reader
unacquainted with Powys's writings as a whole would assume
from a selection of representative generalisations that he lacks
the 'nobler' or the 'romantic' or the 'true' idea of love. It is
not, obviously, a black-and-white matter. Disenchantment is
not the same thing as cynicism; it is likely to appear as cynicism
only to the blurred-minded, to the self-deceived, and of course
to the cynical. And in any case the health or wisdom of Powys's
outlook is to be judged not so much by the propositions he puts
forward as by the statements made by the works in their
wholeness as art-expression; his 'art-speech' says so much more
than his *dicta*. In their totality the writings show that as well as
possessiveness, cruelty, self-enhancement without scruples, love
comprehends also a human warmth and passion, respect,
tenderness, compassion.

It is not possible by the assembling of even a large number
of Powys's utterances on transience, death, the relation of life
and death, to give more than an approximate impression of the
main stream of his thought on these matters. The matters are
vast and complex, the utterances inevitably self-contradictory.
Moreover, here as elsewhere, if we were endeavouring to
present anything like a full account of the author's 'general
thought' we should have the delicate task of distilling it from
the organic wholes of the stories; the wisdom of Lawrence's
advice, 'Never trust the artist, trust the tale', would again and
again come home to us. All that is possible in the way of
suggesting that main stream—if such a thing exists—is to
present a number of ideas which in one form or another appear
frequently in the writings.

The everlasting recurrence of things, as time passes, is a
preoccupation of Powys's thought:

> A week is a long time. During a week the pains of
> labour may come upon a woman, the babe may be
> born, its name chosen, and the child carried to church

to be baptized. A girl may be courted, married, and be sorry for it during the same period of time. Shepherd Brine may buy a new pair of boots, kick one of the soles off upon the threshold of his own door, and be as bootless as before, in one week. Within a week a man may be taken ill, may suffer sadly, may die, and be buried. (*Unclay*).

And in a sense all life is deception, though even if we come to see death as the only reality we still have the chance of making life full:

It is all pretence, for when no one knows what truth is, what else is there to do but to pretend. All life is pretence, but never death.

That state stands as the one stone unturned in the fields of folly. In all other matters the world is as we like to make it, for not Jesus alone can turn water into wine. A tiny pool may seem the whole of the wine-dark deep, and Mr. Hayhoe's back garden can be a wild wilderness—as indeed it is. (*Unclay*).

How shall we live in a self-devouring yet everlasting universe?

All thought in Dodder was quieted. Still waters covered all motion, and no mental webs were being spun there that bring false hope to man. To grow like the field flowers, what else could man do? To bloom in the summer, to eat of the season's joy and then drink the dark wine of the sadness of the earth during the fall. To breathe again, perhaps, when the winter's sleep is ended. To awake like a leaf to the new season. To exist as a creature of the earth for a moment, what more should be needed?

The evening gnats quivered and danced in the warm air, unmindful of danger. The swallows caught them and they heeded not the act. The tiny pig-louse that lived in the grass upon Madder Hill ate its prey. Then it rolled up into a ball to sleep near an anthill, and was eaten itself. A frog, seeking amusement, hopped out of Joe Bridle's pond, only to find a grave in the cold body of a snake.

> Life and Death do not quarrel in the fields. They are always changing places in the slow dance. Alive here and dead there. So the evening is devoured by the night, and the dawn by the day.　(*Unclay*).

Life is 'cruel', then; often the tormented have to live through it, and even death may not be liberation:

> Sometimes we wonder, when those who live in fear and torment, those who are tainted with a sad and lasting distemper of the mind, are not removed from their sorrows and dreads, by the hand who is supposed to rule the world, more quickly than the usual slow-moving cruelty of life allows.

> But wonder though we may, the bitter things that are written against some trembling ones have to be lived through to the end, be that end near or far, or ever the great day of liberation comes. And even this liberation, that some look forward to so kindly, may for aught we know be but a change of scene : the mere rounding of a point in the sea of time, where the memory of the old woes will beget again new torments, to be remembered again, and new-begotten again, through all eternity.

> 　　　　　　　　　　　　　　(*Innocent Birds*).

This possibility, however, is not often suggested by Powys. A more characteristic view, THE view of death in Powys, is that which sees death as release:

> Upon this side, the folly of passion, sorrow, suffering and pain: every moment merged into the next, and all time passing away like the shadow of a swiftly moving cloud over Madder Hill. Upon the other side, the sweet silence of God.　(*Unclay*).

Nevertheless the fear of death is always close to the surface of men's consciousness:

> Nothing in this world can so terrify a group of

simple people, each more nervous than the other,
than a knock at the back door.

It may be, and I daresay that this is the case, that
we fancy that any knock, even though we think we
know who the knocker really is, may be the post that
we all wot of, that is to call us hence once and for
ever. (*Mockery Gap*).

And the horror is felt the more in contrast with a striking
manifestation of life's beauty:

Summer weather, though our joys are heightened
by the clear and plenteous shining of the sun, cannot
lift the dark shadow of the cloud of death when it is
near; but rather the summer darkens the horror by the
very beauty of its shining. (*Mockery Gap*).

Ultimately, however, when he is inculcating an attitude it is
acceptance that prevails:

'We are all ugly things sometimes, dear Solly, but
let us think of our earthly bed as a safe hiding-place
from all our ugliness—blessed be His name.'

Mrs. Crocker sat down upon the grass and looked
at a daisy.

'To an old woman, this mortal life—all that is left of
it—is closing upon every side; and we are forced to
bow down nearer and ever nearer to the earth. But
look at this daisy, Solly; it knows its times and
seasons.'

Mrs. Crocker looked up at a hedge where two
children in white frocks were picking May blossom.

'Who would wish to be called Mrs. Crocker, or
even Deborah Crocker, for ever?' she said, smiling.
'And poor Crocker always felt his name such a
burden.' (*Innocent Birds*).

Mr. Vardy, the cobbler in *God*, offers a conclusion, but not
necessarily final and rigid, which we may take as Powys's:

. . . to accept the better and the worse, that is
wisdom. To see the wicked and the good with the

same understanding, to watch all the worlds and all life flowing into nothingness and yourself with it, with no foolish mournings, that is wisdom.

'To sit solitary, to make our bed in the dew of the morning, to welcome the woman and the adder into our garden of love, to welcome the grave as the true state of joy, that is the way to live, a companion of the wise.'

All Mr. Vardy's wrinkles were laughing together.

One of the great germinating truths for Powys is the bond between man and earth:

Dost thou see the valley before thee? Fair and fruitful are the palm trees in the valley, thy love hangeth over them and thou willest to become them. Thou goest forth and diggest in the valley and plantest seed; it springeth up and the rain nourisheth it, and the winds pass over it. The fruit groweth ripe and thou takest it into thy body to nourish thee, and it passeth from thee again into the ground. The earth that is in thee and around thee loveth thee and calleth thee ever to her bosom. (*An Interpretation of Genesis*).

This bond is for all:

No one who ever comes to Dodder escapes the old spider, whose invisible web binds him tightly, a web not altogether unholy, which holds a man to the earth, that at the last—and let us gather no more sorrow than we can bear—unravels the web and delivers the man to Death. (*Unclay*).

Man is ruled, in general, by the 'mob' of instincts and desires that struggle for expression in him:

One can see, while writing odd things about oneself, that inside the mob still rules, just as it does outside in the world. And the mob may be rioting quite merrily under a policeman's jacket, or corrupting innocence under lawn sleeves in a cathedral. I think that the mob—I know them, even hidden in a snug English village—I think that the mob will always

rule; for it is by the law of hate and not by the law
of love that the world lives and has its being.

                              (*Soliloquies of a Hermit*).

Individual living is possible, but the individual has a tre-
mendously difficult struggle with the herd, the herd of which
he himself is part, and whose underlying motivating force he
himself at least in part, shares:

> We go about the world being friendly, but the mob
> always tells us where to go, and how to confine our
> friendliness to the railway carriage, and our morals
> to our homes. The mob soon breaks our windows, if
> we do not behave after its manner. All our little
> moral sensations are upon the surface of our lives; it is
> the great immoralist that lies beneath.

                              (*Soliloquies of a Hermit*).

Deception and self-deception are rife; when the Rev. Hector
Turnbull, in *Mr. Tasker's Gods*, calls out his son's name,

> The tone of his voice was sleek and moist, disclosing
> the fact, unknown to the doctors, that every man has
> poison glands under his tongue, and when he speaks
> most gently he is really making up his mind to use
> them.

The thoughts of the same gentleman, as he walked home after
rebuking the new school-teacher because her blouse was too
gay for the national school, 'were the thoughts of a male
hyena'. But it behoves us not to be superior in our virtue.
We are all subject to

> those rude little hits that life gives when we least expect
> them, turning us from calm, quiet, steady Christians
> into outrageous and blood-thirsty Turks.

                              (*Mr. Tasker's Gods*).

*An Interpretation of Genesis* has much to say about man's desire
for power:

> Those that slay the king with the sword, do they not
> desire to reign in his stead?

and

> Man's folly is that he loveth himself before the heaven
> and the earth.

Many men upon earth, and Christ in particular, have seen and shown that a life other than one of self-aggrandisement is possible, but instinct is all too often more powerful than moral idealism:

> man loveth the beast that is behind him more than
> the son of man that is before.

The 'goodly words' of the preacher are a danger to truth:

> Full of pleasant words is the preacher, and the
> desire for goodly words is in man; man seeketh him
> that can speak goodly words. Lo, a wonderful thing
> is this, the preacher standing in a white garment, and
> a multitude of people gathered together; the desire of
> all these and the desire of the preacher is for goodly
> words.
>
> The multitude give ear to the preacher and they
> say to one another,
> 'Hath he not wisdom? is not God with him?'
> The goodly words of the preacher are let loose
> upon all men, and men come together to hear them.
> To say the thing that shall please men, that is the
> desire of the preacher, and because of this desire the
> preacher, yea, and his hearers also, shall come to
> the place of darkness.

With these ideas of man's nature and ways it is not surprising to come across such phrases as 'the vice of action', and 'ignorance, that black monster', and as natural corollaries, 'the holy and blessed thought of an everlasting peace', and 'the supreme loveliness of lonely silence'. But an unquestioned assent to the generalisations and abstractions of Powys would be little more enlightening than a similar attitude to the 'beauties' of Shakespeare or the 'wise sayings' of George Eliot. Nevertheless, one of the fertilising feeling-ideas of the stories is that of the achievement of peace, the escape from tumult and confusion into peace, and this is also perhaps the central single

thought which is likely to remain with us as the product of the
generalisations. Certainly disenchantment and pessimism are
key themes in discussion of Powys. And it is a fact that the
dark-toned, 'pessimistic' generalizations far outnumber the
'hopeful' ones. But it can be repeated that the art is an
infinitely more complex affair than the sum of the abstracted
thoughts. Powys's art forces us to a revision of our notions of
pessimism. Like tragedy, it is, ultimately, for and not against
life. Life is troubled, and death is a release; but life is rich.
'We are doomed to live,' wrote Lawrence, in whom the
reverence for life never failed.

*Chapter Eight*

# THEODORE POWYS

THOUGH ultimately the flame is perhaps nameless, it is made of something: behind and in the writer's words are the things which have been the most deeply formative for him, themes and preoccupations consciously selected and emphasised and engaging the range of feelings they do engage. Previous chapters may have indicated something of the 'flame' of Theodore Powys, something which when we say 'Powysian' will suggest not idiosyncratic devices or obsessions or mannerisms but a profound individuality, the individuality which has been nourished by a deep, constant interest in life.

Different kinds and manifestations of love, their dangers and their delights; death, both fearsome and a haven; gossip, spite, cruelty, avarice, snobbery; gentleness, kindly odd humour, integrity in judgment, joy in contemplation: in general terms these are some of the main themes and attributes that Powys deals with. For symbols and images there are clouds, storms, the sun, books, bed, a bottle to drink from, soil, farmyard muck, ponds, Madder Hill and the solitary figure often seen upon it, gusts of wind, footsteps, waves of the sea, their infinite number and their sound, a flower in its singleness, a glow-worm, buttercup meadows. This (far from comprehensive) enumeration of themes and symbols is offered mainly to suggest the commonness of the items, and clearly in itself it cannot be very specifically suggestive. Nor could an attempted brief summary of technique give more than a rough idea of the way in which what we think of as familiar is transformed into illuminating art. It is possible, as we have seen, to speak of success through the use of the utmost simplicity of language, of success with the uniquely ordered sequences of short sentences and short paragraphs, with tightly packed dialogue conveying complexities and shades with symbol and repeated image, with unexpected juxtapositions and changes of direction; but finally it is only through the manner in which these and other things function *together* in the individual works that we are enabled to catch something of the essence of the 'flame'.

The life of rural quietness that Powys elected to live was perfectly in consonance with his artistic purposes. For he is not an explorer of specifically twentieth-century civilisation. His writing is remarkable for the paucity in it of the external accoutrements, the economic-social machinery of the age. Yet he is unmistakably *of* the age. He is modern—the paradox is only a seeming one—in his very insistence on the everlasting elements beneath the masks and behaviour-vicissitudes of human life. And in being a witness to certain central deep-seated traits and habits in human beings he not only recalls Wordsworth's famous remarks about the essential passions of men being more observable in a rural environment, but also often reveals ideas and a way of thinking which recall for instance Freud, or Sir James Frazer. His success as an artist is of course the irrefutable proof that he has not simply taken over the conclusions of psychologist and anthropologist. With his gallery of human types he deals with the immemorial morality-play of life, and much of what he has to say about love and death has behind it both traditional sanctions and modern findings. Many of the stories are marvellously clear and—even though complex—sure statements. But the whole

character of the man as we know it from his life and his writings
is of the kind that we are likely to think of now as simple and
now as complicated.

In his everyday living, for example, there is the matter of
his church-going. This may not have any very great importance
for us now, but it was clearly important to Powys. We cannot
help wondering, in view of the frequency of his biting portrayals
of clergymen and his ironic references to ritual, as well as his
general attitude to conventional morality, why he read the
lessons at East Chaldon church for nearly forty years. It was
not because family tradition demanded it; most of the Powyses
rebelled against the father's orthodoxies when the spirit moved
them. I thought it would be interesting to ask for an opinion
about T.F.'s church-going from one or two people who were
closely connected with him. His son Francis Powys, his brother
John Cowper Powys, and his life-long friend Louis Wilkinson
(Marlow), replied fully to my question, which was this: 'Can
you suggest, in view of his general attitude to life and his
expressed anti-clericalism etc., why T.F. Powys was a regular
church-goer?' I quote from the replies in their letters, which
all belong to 1956:

> *From Louis Wilkinson:* I think T. F. P.'s attendances at
> church and his taking Communion are accounted for
> by his sympathy with the Church as a traditional
> influence in English life, a valuable corrective to
> modern changes, modern iconoclasms, and modern
> vulgarities and ugliness. He was certainly not an
> orthodox believer, though he was profoundly religious.
> I guess that he wanted to co-operate with the
> influences of the Church of England as some ancient
> Greeks and Romans wished to co-operate with the
> accepted religious influences of their day. They would
> throw incense on the altars of the gods because they
> believed that belief in them was to the good generally,
> and that established religion, however mythical, was
> better than no established religion. Also, T. F. P.

K

enjoyed going to church. He would never have gone
merely from a sense of duty.

*A second letter from Louis Wilkinson:* A few days ago
I was talking to a friend of T. F. P.'s on this subject,
and she told me that he told her more than once that
he enjoyed going to church. Also he said that, if he
didn't go to these weekday services, there would be no
one to make the responses. My own experience bears
this out, for I went with him several times and we were
the only members of the congregation. This friend
(Mrs. Donald Gill) thought that T. F. P., as a
clergyman's son, felt at home in church, that
attendance at services revived childhood memories,
satisfied a kind of nostalgia. She said that, as a
clergyman's daughter, she could sympathise here,
although she is no more orthodox than T. F. P. was.
I give this suggestion for what it is worth; it is another
guess. It might also be taken into account that he was
on friendly terms with the clergyman, and may have
gone to church partly (but I am sure only partly)
on that account.

*From John Cowper Powys:* I am delighted to hear of your
book on Theodore and you couldn't have done better
than to ask this particular question of his nearest
relations and friends. . . . Here is what I say at once
and with so little hesitation that I write it straight
down. Theodore took the Sacrament for the same
reason that he went to church because he instinctively
felt that in regard to the ultimate problem—is there a
God and if there is just what are we going to do and
feel about it?—it was wisest and best to be on what
might be called *the safe side.*

*Again from John Cowper Powys:* I thought it might
interest you if I added one more view of Theodore's
pleasure in going to church, namely that of my
American friend Miss Playter who has been my

companion for more than thirty years. Here is what she says. Theodore was the most original of the Powys family and his originality was such that it inevitably isolated him even from his closest friends and relations. And in order to have another original Being for his companion *he concentrated on God*. His God was like himself and was anything but the God discussed by theologians. Theodore's God had nothing to do with Jesus or the Holy Ghost or the Virgin. He was companion *Other to Theodore*, an *Alter Ego* for him. He loved being in church because it was the dwelling of this other self, this other eccentric, this other original, who was the Only Being who understood him and whom he understood. The Sacrament was just incidental to his fondness for Church as the dwelling of his only Alter Ego, his only Other Self, and no doubt it satisfied the *Major domo* of his Friend's House to see him accept the Sacrament. I mean it pleased the clergyman. I must confess that what my American friend says strikes me as more likely to be one truth than anything his brothers and even his sisters could say, because as the old proverb puts it: Onlookers see most of the game.

*From Francis Powys:* I wish I could help with the problem of Theodore's church-going. Certainly he was deeply religious in a simple way. I think his later church-going was some sort of preparation for death which when it did arrive he was completely ready for. When asked by Alyse (wife of Llewelyn Powys) why he went to church when he said he didn't believe in it, he replied that it was the only place he could go to be really quiet. I went with him once to Compline in Mappowder church. We were the only two there. He said to me, 'I do it to please old Frank' (the Vicar). Lord, I just don't know, I suppose. I think he had a sort of simple eighteenth-century belief that gave him

pleasure and courage. I don't think it's possible to
explain . . . There was a period of course that he
went through of terrible depression, and he was
always haunted by the fear of poverty— for his family,
I think. He himself wasn't interested in money. Those
times left their mark on him, until perhaps the last
twelve years or so.

It seems impossible to extract from this quantity of interesting
and varied opinion and testimony an impelling central motive
for Powys's church-going. In conversation with me Mrs.
Violet Powys has stressed her husband's inherited religious
tendency and his love of the quiet of the church.

Whatever in his deepest being he retained or discarded of
interest in Church custom and observance, he possessed in
marked degree certain qualities that we especially connect with
Christianity and other religions and systems of thought:
humility, for instance. The humility of Powys was real; it was
not, as humility often is, a willed self-abasement with ulterior
motives conscious or unconscious. It was quite without
ostentation, and it consorted easily with the solitary pride of
genius. It is shown in his easy moving among everyday
domesticities (both in his life and in his writings) as it is shown
in his recognition of non-human forces, his lack of pretension
and his complete unsnobbishness, his quiet profound worship
of natural beauty—'worship' really has a meaning here—of the
sun, of the night, of the soil with its worms, its decaying bodies,
its daisies. He stands in general for things that the majority do
not care for: satisfaction with few amenities and goods,
contemplation in quietness, positive pleasure in idleness,
profound moral interests. Mrs. Powys has told me that when
they were living in the tiny cottage next to the church at
Mappowder, T. F. having by then become known, they would
be visited on occasion by certain 'literary' people whom he
did not care for. He did not want lionising, and on their
approach, if he had time he would quietly climb out of the
window on the blind side and silently walk away down the

lane. Normally, however, his behaviour towards visitors was gracious.

The pessimistic element in Powys's outlook comes of course from his belief in the existence of certain innate and (frequently) intractable qualities in man. It would be a simplification to speak of Original Sin, or of the Seven Deadly Sins, or of mechanistic determinism, and to leave it at that, but it is nonetheless a fact that both his inheritance and his personal observation of life, or rather perhaps the two working together, tended to lead him to conclusions like this:

> Whatever can in any way stem the horrid waters of
> rude and hideous violence, has done and will ever do
> . . . the greatest good to man. (*Unclay*).

Negative as the attitude may appear to us, we should find ourselves hard put to it to deny wholly the justice of the opinion. There is of course a positive side to this lauding of respite, expressing itself not only in the joys of solitude and idleness—

> Beside the pond, lying idly with his feet in the sun
> and his head shaded, was the new fisherman. He lay
> upon the soft moss and clover in indulgent ease,
> looking now at Mr. Cuddy's ducks and now upwards
> through the sweetest and most delightful of rich
> green leaves— (*Mockery Gap*)

but in meditation and the rigours of thought. There are photographs and drawings of Powys where mouth and eyes suggest considerable strain. But despite his chosen withdrawal from 'the world' he was the antithesis of Hawthorne's Ethan Brand, who wandered the world on a quest for the Unpardonable Sin and found it finally in his own heart, turned to stone while he was everlastingly engaged in observing the hearts of others. Powys never uses evil in order to feed upon the pleasures of exposure. It was as much his burden and task as anyone's to resolve the conflict between the impulse of kindness and the impulse to surrender to disgust with humanity, but his sympathies never atrophied. It was no mock-modesty that caused him to say that of the photographs which had been taken of him he disliked least the one that is reproduced as the frontispiece of this book; he said it looked like a shepherd.

While offering in his finest work a profound wisdom-through-disenchantment, he is also for pleasure and a greater freedom. But never in any platform manner; Powys has no programme. On the contrary he represents a warning against the follies of an ignorant optimism and against insufficiently based schemes for human betterment. But he does speak for enjoyment. The frequent sexual innuendoes in his writings are not gross but playful (except where they are by intention sinister): it is not pornographic whimsy but a gesture towards warmth and love when Nellie breaks off the green seed-pod—'phallic' and beautiful, though Powys doesn't tell us this—of a yellow-horn poppy and throws it at Mr. Pattimore. Beneath the gay wantonness of many of Powys's references to physical love is a concern for warmth and real feeling in relationship. While not exploring this theme with Lawrence's insight and pertinacity, the accumulative effect of his writings shows him to be 'modern' in his intelligent liberal approval—though never forgetting the possible pitfalls and adulterations—of physical pleasure.

He is of our time too, or rather in advance of it, in his concern for the status of women; though 'status' with its associations of equal pay and social emancipation and so on, seems hardly the right word. Powys's interest is in the fundamentals of the position which the scheme of things as it is and the nature of men as they are seem to make inevitable for women. The substance of the generalities of the following quotation from *The Two Thieves* is conveyed through the action and dialogue of a good many of the novels and stories:

> Within the circle drawn by Pride, Cruelty may frolic.
> Cruelty has many ways of inflicting torments upon
> men and women. The crude tortures of Ivan the
> Terrible only represent a few of them. Often in a
> household where all seems to be well, there Cruelty

walks. When God devised the act of procreation, Cruelty demanded a share of the fun. She said that, without her, nothing could be made. God was aware of the truth of this, and so Cruelty came into the world. Cruelty knew at once where and how she could most amuse herself. In the married state, if the woman be docile and loving, the man, being the stronger of the two, has power to do as he chooses, and she will never dare to tell her friends or her servants what she suffers. Cruelty is a fine artist, the ten thousand bites that she gives to her victim do not kill, because each bite is allowed to heal up before another is given. In a woman there are two things that may be tortured—her body and her mind. The man may go on his way, rejoicing, whatever he does to her. A jovial look will excuse all guile.

Perhaps the force and persistence in Powys of the feeling and ideas present in that passage was a cause of what to my mind is a marked lack in his work: he clearly was not interested in attempting any presentation of a marital relationship between intelligent people. The lack doesn't affect his finest writings; they are achieved and complete in themselves. And it would be irrelevant to complain of the absence of anything like Lawrentian portrayal and exploration. But the introduction of such a relationship, in the Powysian type-manner—one feels that he could have done it—would have added significantly to the range of the vision he offers.

Powys did not cling to his 'narrow' life in an isolated village because he was concerned to record the passing of what we broadly call rural modes. There is less of that particular element, as a main theme, in his work than there is in Hardy, who was older than he, to say nothing of Lawrence, who was ten years younger. Nevertheless, writing mostly in a period remarkable for technical innovators more and less important— Lawrence and Eliot, Joyce and Virginia Woolf—he is English in his settings and his spirit alike. There is the numerousness of

the observed details: the bramble leaves made shiny by the
winter fog, the bottoms of the thatcher's shoes (seen as he sits
on the ancient corn-bin in Mark Only's barn) pressed into
ridges by the rounds of the ladder which he climbs daily, the
little spotted pigs that run grunting, in a high state of
excitement, in the lanes, the dampness that is long retained in
the knots of the cornstalks. There is the recording, in almost
all his writings, of the time of the year, a feeling of the seasons
which recalls Edward Thomas: 'Two swifts flashed past her,
a cuckoo called—its note was changed, summer was come.'
There are the described externals, though almost always
briefly described, of the country scene: barn, church, inn,
fields, cottages, and so on. On another level there are the
people he deals with, and their destiny to return to the earth
and be 'dry bones in Madder'. These and other things belong
organically to the novels and stories. The feeling of tradition is
strong. There are frequent reminders of what has gone. In a
passage of *Unclay* we are told of the country sounds that are no
longer or only rarely heard near Madder Hill, the trotting of
the horse with gig along the turnpike road, the cries of the
curlew and the raven. When you hear the thuds of a carpet
being beaten, it may be

> enough to awaken the remembrance of older times.
> One shuts one's eyes and enters a barn. The dust flies,
> there is a smell of dry straw.
>
> Two men are at work with flails. One of them—
> John Sherwood, who wears side-whiskers—wields
> dexterously a strange weapon, steadily beating a
> heap of beans—dry and black—that are stacked in
> the barn. Presently the black stalks are taken up and
> the beans sifted and placed in sacks. John Sherwood
> drinks from a stone jar.

Memories are vivid in Powys, his thought often turns to the
past. When he refers to the ever-increasing rush and noise of
the world it is always with distaste. His essential Englishness
resides, however, not only in what Dorset means to him but

in his whole character as a man and as a committed literary artist.

Powys is a profoundly English writer because he had much first-hand knowledge of the ancient village life of England and because his disposition, or his destiny, while being unconsciously formed in a measure by what he inherited from masters like Bunyan and the writers of the Bible (to say nothing of Jane Austen), also led him back consciously to these and others when he began to write novels and stories. The references to the Bible, the visible parallels and links, are of course innumerable. Some of the stories are versions of actual Biblical episodes, and no alert reader will fail to see how he uses Biblical phrases and even whole sentences for purposes of ironic inflexion, or humorous parallelism, or reinforcement, or reminder and recall of the formative past with its lessons and warnings. It is one of Daniel's visions (Daniel, chapter VII) that provides the white woolly hair of Mr. Weston; and Mr. Weston's lion is a little the richer when we know the verse from the first Book of Peter, chapter V: 'Be sober, be vigilant; because your adversary the devil, as a roaring lion, walketh about, seeking whom he may devour'.

Bunyan is present not only at the profounder levels of inheritance but also frequently in idiom and method: for example, from *The Two Thieves*, ' . . . Pride thought himself disgraced by such mean lodgings, and went off in a huff'. *The Key of the Field* is in its small way another *Pilgrim's Progress*, containing an actual vivid phrase from Bunyan when a key turns in a lock 'damnable hard'. There is more than one story in which the substitution of a pig for a baby occurs, this being unmistakably prompted by the second Towneley *Shepherd's Play* or some similar folk story; and in the manner of the medieval play Powys mixes fun with serious moral significances; and on occasion suggests, as those plays do, the movement from winter hardness and death and hardness of heart to birth and joy in Christ and spring. Not that the particular stories I have in mind here (*Godfather Dottery* and *The Shut Door*) are

characterised by power. All that I wish to draw attention to is
the presence of a medieval element. It is clear that the shepherd
character with its traditional tenderness and responsibility
and connection with the Nativity appealed deeply to Powys.
Often the shepherd is figured, actual and symbolical, going
about his work, especially at night and under the stars. Carters
also, and clerks, sextons, preachers, ploughmen, come to Powys
down the centuries. When he writes 'He carried an armful of
sticks that he knew would be a welcome gift', he is testifying in
however small a way to a certain ancient-traditional Christian
attitude of charity to the poor. When he quotes in a story the
verse of an old popular song, with its vestiges of medieval sin
and hell comically viewed, we are likewise in touch, tenuously
though it may be, with the past. My justification for calling
that song 'popular' is that I remember having it sung to me,
when a child, by my mother, who came from the Cotswolds.
This is the verse I remember; it is virtually the same as that
given by Powys:

> I am the ghost of Sir John James Christopher
>     Benjamin Binns,
> I was cut off right in the midst of my sins,
> And my home is down below,
> I'm just let up for an hour or so,
> When the cock begins to crow, farewell Benjamin
>     Binns.

Ideas common and important in medieval literature, in
plays, sermons, flyting poems, and bird and beast fables, are
prominent in Powys in a form which often clearly recalls that
literature: the common fate of men, the idea that life is lent
only, or the idea that Death is a thief, the abuse of wealth and
authority, retribution, forgiveness, charity. Then his characters
are sometimes in the 'humour' manner of earlier centuries;
he even has here and there sketches which suggest Earle and
Overbury. Sometimes there is an echo which is readily enough
placed, as when at the end of *Mr. Handy's Wife* Othello comes
to mind as Mr. Handy, overhearing the soldier-talk which

proves him a cuckold, cries 'My wife! my wife!' as he staggers
and falls. At other times the link may be less verbal and more
a matter of spirit and essence: in *Unclay*, where the drinkers at
the Dodder Inn hear in the intervals between their roisterings
the sound of a scythe being sharpened, some readers may pause
and recall that dramatic moment in *The Pardoner's Tale:*

These riotoures thre, of whiche I telle,
Longe erst er prime rong of any belle,
Were set hem in a taverne for to drynke;
And as they sat they herde a belle clynke
Biforn a cors, was caried to his grave.

As a story-telling moralist Powys has a long ancestry in the
English language. Never naïvely prompted by didacticism or
moral fervours, he is an artist-moralist disturbing and delighting
with beauty and power. Whether we call him Christian by
virtue of his compassion or of his more obvious literary forbears
(always remembering that Christianity in medieval literature
and in Bunyan and the Bible is not simply Christianity but
includes much else besides), or of the influence of Calvinism
upon him; or whether he is 'pagan' in his worship of other gods
than the orthodox One, in his liberal attitude towards love,
in his recognition of forces outside man's jurisdiction; or
whether he is modern in his mingling of Christian and pagan
and of Western and Eastern modes of thought: Christian,
pagan, or modern, it doesn't matter. It is his art which holds
the essence of Powys and which has value for us.

The question 'What is pessimism?' is answerable in so many
ways that it is hardly answerable at all. But taking the general
notion of it, would any thoughtful person care to say that
Powys, with all his violences, his depicted horrors of human
behaviour, his 'cynical' utterances, exaggerated? Even if we
put aside the achieved caricature-successes in his work, and
even if we disregard for the moment the counterbalancing light
and peace and the feeling creative mind, should we care to
argue that that part of Powys's world figured by the Meres and
Mumbys and Tulks and Mrs. Vospers represents deeper evils,

and a greater proportion of evil in his presented world, than do
in ours the infinite tortuosities and debasements of politics and
of much popular entertainment and culture, to say nothing of
the enormity of the callousness displayed in the preparation of
mass-destruction devices? Here is a quotation from Bunyan:

> Now there was made in the room hard by a very
> great fire; so the gentleman took up the babe, went
> and drew the coals from the stock, cast the child in and
> covered it up, and there was an end of that.

And this is Conrad:

> We can't return to Nature, since we can't change our
> place in it. Our refuge is in stupidity, in drunkenness
> of all kinds, in lies, in beliefs, in murder, thieving,
> reforming, in negation, in contempt—each man
> according to the promptings of his particular devil.

This is admittedly one of Conrad's darkest utterances, and
admittedly too the quoted Bunyan is not inclusively
representative. Nonetheless neither quotation is singular; the
author of each was aware—to understate it—of the tremendous
power of the forces of irrationality and rationalisation in
human character, aims, and conduct. We do not care to let
our minds dwell on the amount of cruelty in the world, personal
cruelty open or hidden, but mostly hidden, and 'mass'-cruelty
obscured and gilded by professed idealism. Powys can no more
be called a depressing writer than Bunyan or Conrad; and no
one arraigns the author of *King Lear*—'Out, vile jelly!'—for
cruelty. Instances of cruelty are abundant in Powys precisely
because he was most painfully aware of its universality. When
he generalises about it the note is likely to be one of bitter but
controlled concern (as in the passage from *The Two Thieves*
previously quoted in this chapter), and at the farthest remove
from unconscious indulgence.

It is not being paradoxical to suggest that some readers
might be disposed to see Powys's writing primarily as comedy.
Certainly he makes us vividly aware of the comic possibilities
of (in his own words) 'a very strange show indeed, the inhabited

world'. Even *The Bucket and the Rope*, even *The Barometer*, are in a sense comic. That by the depth of his concern and commitment he is, ultimately, a tragic writer, indicates how the comic can be assimilated into the tragic. But it is worth glancing here at the overt and specific comedy element in our attempt to get a reasonably complete impression of the man and the writer. The humour he gets from his occasional use of the disguise convention is usually lightly pleasant but does not often reach the level of the Mrs. Tubb parts of *Kindness in a Corner*, where re-readings reveal a series of neat correspondences and amusing *doubles entendres*. The right note is hit for the conclusion of this novel: Canon Dibben, sensual and erring, he who had always preached the dangers to the soul of the 'leprosy of unchastity', had been hiding in a cupboard in the hope of discovering a secret sin of the Rev. Dottery, and had been caught in the seat of his trousers by a hook belonging to the fishing-tackle which Mr. Dottery had shoved in thirty years before; Lottie, the maid, meets Mr. Dottery on the stairs:

'Even though Canon Dibben do drink,' she said reproachfully, ' 'e be a clergyman, and great hook do hurt him sadly.'

'I hope not,' said Mr. Dottery, and went at once to the study to release the wonderful fish. As soon as he had freed him, Mr. Dottery said happily:

'I trust, Mr. Dibben, that you will breakfast with me—there are fried soles.'

'I prefer toast,' said Mr. Dibben angrily.

The farcical element is absorbed in the easy humour and wit of Mr. Dottery's allusion to the state of soul of the caught fish. Something has already been said of the humour and wit attaching to certain key characters like John Death and the fisherman; of the sardonic comic-tragic note of many of the Fables and stories; of the particular flavour of his characters in the flat, the types and grotesques who have a long line of ancestors in our literature.

These and other notes are struck again and again. The quiet

moralising of the speech of the manager of the town burial-
board as he shows Mr. Dobbin round the cemetery has
something of a Shakespearian tone (Hamlet on occasions, and
Posthumous's gaoler):

> 'Nothing disturbs our peace here,' said Mr. Best; 'our
> guests are all silent ones, and whatever noise they
> made before they came, they are quiet now.'

There are innumerable incidental ironic touches:

> . . . the consecrated ground, that is to say, the
> ground upon which the magic feet of the Bishop—
> who bought his boots at Jeffrey's in the Strand—
> had trod.

There is preposterous joking, as this from the sadist-seducer,
Bugby:

> ' 'Tis religion,' said Bugby, looking at Polly's young
> strong legs, 'that do hurt they maidens.'

Of the longer works, only *Kindness in a Corner* could be
classified as comedy, but there is a large number of short
humorous tales. Many of these, as I have previously suggested,
are flimsy, though sometimes amusing in their farce and
ingeniousness. Never merely crude or uproarious—even though
'Circe' Truggin, the sexton, 'applies his wand' (a stout stick)
to the avaricious farmer who has lapped up from the trough
the ale especially bought for Mr. Dottery's pigs—they are
often lightly and pleasantly strengthened with ideas and
ponderable questions. A good example is *Old Men*, where a gay
and charitable spirit is thrown neatly over an up-to-date rural
version of Susanna and the Elders. The 'wicked' love-making
and the lying are here seen not only as harmless but as aids to
warmth and friendliness. The varied ingredients of the story
—the gentle old men and the merry servant, celandines, wifely
shrewishness, cows in the meadow, talk of Kant and Bishop
Berkeley and Truth, Mr. Topp's black-and-white sow, Calvary,
the sermon about 'the wickedness of wanton dalliance that
leads to worse', boots made yellow by the buttercups—are
controlled by a hand that is skilful, cool, and kindly.

A challenge to put one's finger on the very heart of T. F. Powys could not easily be met; one thing that would come very near the centre would be the combination in him of a consciousness of the power of the forces that animate mankind, and of the dangers of departure from certain moral orthodoxies, with a tolerance and sometimes a forceful approval of 'sin' as it is theologically or ecclesiastically or conventionally understood. The length of the supporting quotation that follows is due to the need to show how Powys is developing his immediate theme:

In the village everyone continued to be just as interested as they had been the week before in the all-important subjects of sin and repentance. For Mr. Hayhoe had certainly stirred the hearts of the people by describing in his sermon—his text was 'Behold, I have prepared my dinner'—how full of contentment is a true penitent when he has confessed his trouble.

Even the older men began to be interested in what was being talked about, and Joe White's father—a man with a rough beard and a strong hand for a spade —stopped Mr. Bunny on his way to the Inn, to observe, in an extremely melancholy tone, that he believed that he had done something very ill, though he was not sure whether a sin that was certainly very dreadful in his own eyes would appear as bad in the eyes of a gentleman like Mr. Hayhoe.

'I wouldn't like to offend 'e by going,' said Mr. White, 'for perhaps 'e mid think I were only coming to vestry to make fun of 'e.'

'What is it thee've been and done, neighbour?' inquired Mr. Bunny; ' 'tain't nothing to do wi' any of they young maidens I don't suppose?'

'No, no,' replied Mr. White carelessly, ' 'tain't for I to talk of they silly doings; 'tis a real wickedness that I be guilty of.'

'Ah!' said Mr. Bunny, 'a green spider walked over me plate at breakfast-time, and so I did know that I would hear something curious when supper came.'

'Then I suppose I must tell thee,' said Mr. White, 'though what be done will sound a mortal sin to the green trees. Thee do know how poor they spring onions of mine do look for the time of year?'

'I have noticed them,' replied Mr. Bunny, 'and I have often wondered how they came to be so bad. I have never seen so poor a crop in your garden, neighbour, for many a long year.'

'I did forget to dung the ground,' said Mr. White, in a low and troubled tone.

Mr. Bunny stood back a pace or two in horror.

'I never thought 'twould be as bad as that,' he remarked feelingly. 'But haven't thee any excuse to offer to the good clergyman, anything that mid save thee from the wrath of God? For, if thee do carry thik sad tale of sin to church, 'tain't no forgiveness that thee be likely to have, for surely 'tis the sin against the Holy Ghost that thee've been and done. For what can be worse than to starve thee's own poor ground, and to deny, through thee's carnal forgetfulness, the proper yearly bread to a poor dumb onion? I do much fear that Mr. Hayhoe will look grimly at thee, and will shout out, "To hell wi'thee, unprofitable servant, where the teeth do gnash, and bones do boil!" Though 'tis to be hoped that thee can say something to turn the wrath aside.'

'I fear that I can think of nothing,' answered Mr. White, rubbing his head in great perplexity, 'unless to say that I were drunk every night for a fortnight before I sowed they unlucky seeds, and did go each of they nights out into farmer's meadow with Mrs. Wicks.'

' 'Twouldn't do to take thik silly tale to church,'

observed Mr. Bunny, 'for God would only make sport
of 'ee for telling 'en.'

'Then I be damned,' said Mr. White sadly.

This passage from *The Only Penitent*, with its humour and its
interesting overtones, belongs to the same story that gives us
the force and the tragic implications of the meeting between
Mr. Hayhoe and Tinker Jar. Humorous disregard of orthodox
moral values—if we don't laugh Powys has written in vain—
goes with a deeply searching moral interest. Powys can afford
to mock the letter because he knows what the spirit is. He is
never priggish in this knowledge.

Evidence of the range and kind of his literary knowledge,
his 'culture', is likewise there for our picking up; it is never
thrust on us. Sometimes it occurs in passing references which
have no very great significance in themselves as enriching
agents but which add a little to the particular atmosphere of
the book or of a character, as when the flavour of Mr. Dottery's
learning is suggested by mention here and there of Anacreon,
Lucan, Erasmus's letters in Latin to Henry VIII, and so on.
Powys's shelves held many classics from many languages. He
was well read in the great philosophers and he seems to have
at least sampled pretty well everything in English poetry
except the contemporary. He often valued a book for the sense
it gave of the living man who wrote it:

> I like the whole man in his work—his body, his hands
> and his eyes, and even his belly. And I like best to
> read of actual moving, working life; of ships as Conrad
> writes of them, or anything else that has a real touch
> of moving, itching, speaking life about it. Let me have
> the whole body of the man as well as his brain in his
> book.

So certain smaller books were of absorbing interest to him:
Wesley's Journal is 'intensely human . . . he let the winds of
heaven into his life, the sly old heathen! . . . John Bunyan
would have called Wesley a cock of the right kind.' It is the
sense of the passion of life that he mainly feels in the Bible: a

L

fine paragraph in the *Soliloquies*, beginning with a quiet
understatement—'Another book that sometimes pleases me,
and I like the sober colour of its binding, is the Bible'—conveys
the excitement which its varied beauty and terror bring to him,
and shows how utterly un-pious was his approach: 'And how
well it keeps to the earth and the things of the earth, the poetry
of the belly of life.' Culpeper's *Herbal*, also about things of the
earth and the work of a man of independence, courage, and
kindness, was a favourite book of Powys. So was Law's *Serious
Call to a Devout and Holy Life*. Law was a man of simple life,
charitable to the point of incurring rebuke from the rector,
shrewd as well as mystical, actively kind to animals, *and*
outrageously puritanical in his view of enjoyment. Powys
enjoyed the grotesque mixture that Law was. Mr. Weston is
glad to find that Luke Bird reads the *Serious Call* (he is glad also
to bring the joy of physical love to Luke and Jenny). Allusions
of this latter sort are of course richly suggestive in their context
and not at all arbitrary. But it is rather significant that almost
all Powys's named references to writers are to writers of the
past. Despite the frequency of the kind of explicit idea which
relates him at certain points to (say) Freud:

> But though they wished to do mischief, their efforts
> were futile, because the fear that they had of one
> another compelled a better behaviour,

and at another point to Frazer:

> In the common lives of people, one power is always
> waiting ready to drive out another, in order to rule
> in its place. There is always a stronger one coming.
> Each guardian of the temple is slain in his turn, then
> the victor becomes priest in his stead. Power that
> conquers power is the order of all our lives, but who is
> it that dare name the last power to kill? What will
> He do, when the fatal blow is struck, and he becomes
> lord of the temple, with no rival to challenge His
> victory?
> With no power above Him, with no power higher

than Himself, what can He do? Will He—in order
to complete the conquest—slay Himself? Will He
listen too, like our poor drunkards—for in all that
temple there will be silence? Shall He hear again
the many trampling feet of a new generation of men,
or will the last enemy destroy him too? Will God die?

(*Unclay*)

—despite this evidence of a 'modern' knowledge and spirit,
the persistency with which he held to his seclusion made certain
limitations inevitable. Considering what he deliberately cut
himself off from, and to what extent he narrowed his outward
life-experience, it is astonishing that he accomplished so much.
But he did deprive himself of the possibility of exploring the
changing consciousness of the age, the course of history and
civilisation. By the side of Tolstoy, of Lawrence, he is bound
to appear restricted.

Perhaps Hawthorne provides a not unjust comparison. In
some particulars indeed, both those of the external kind and
those having a bearing on essence and stature, the resem-
blances are quite striking. Living quiet and outwardly un-
eventful lives and having little contact with the literary world,
both are allegorists, but with a strong infusion of local colour
and feeling and a certain everyday robustness. Both (though
Hawthorne probably in greater measure) have to contend
with a heritage of gloomy Calvinistic determinism, and the
best work of each comes from the way that the often dark
material takes on beautiful colouring in the artist's vision and
hands. When they sink below their best, as they often do,
it is likely to be through over-insistence and repetitiveness
or over-ingeniousness. Their breadth in their best writings is
that of a generous spirit and a free play of mind within a restricted area, rather than that of the greatest writer's abound-
ing perceptiveness of variety.

But when all is said, and when any comparison one may
choose to make has been made, T. F. Powys is a strengthening
antidote—and it is 'strengthening' I would emphasise here—

not only to intellectuality of the arid kind but also to the
follies of our times. His writing, while rarely analysing those
times in their palpable manifestations—and I am not forgetting
that the best of it was done in the nineteen-twenties—
nevertheless contains an implicit exposure of them while
reflecting certain aspects of the nature of humanity at all times.
The spirit in which the exposure is made, now bitter and now
compassionate, is salutary because it comes from a mind that
is aware of what really exists, aware of the reality below the
appearance, and aware of possible sources of strength, enjoyment, happiness, and peace.

It is tempting to say that one is glad he did not live to see
the extent of the depredations that were to come—'defence
requirements'—upon the country near the Dorset coast; that
he did not know that the shadow of atomic installations was to
fall over Winfrith (Egdon) Heath, or that myxomatosis was to
do its vicious work over his countryside. But the expression of
such a wish would suggest that the author of *Mr. Weston's Good
Wine* and *Fables* was less tough than we are, and that is not the
case. He was both stronger and more tender.

When the weaknesses of sentimentality and the over-indulged
fancies and the more obvious strains of his writing have been
allowed for, there remains enough of the superlative to enforce
an impression of strength, strength in the superb ordering and
control of a life-experience which, because he saw much,
required much courage. And his acceptance is not of the grim
and stultifying sort; tenderness is always showing itself. It is
seen in the frequency with which he is actively preoccupied
with the theme of genuine loving feeling, in his hatred of
mischievous gossip, in his manner towards small living
creatures. The feeling and attitude that are shown in a letter to
Louis Wilkinson in 1909, when his own children are the
subject, were never destroyed by the disturbing and painful
recognitions that his genius compelled him to:

It is fortunate that you did not choose this present
season for the weather portends no good, whenas in

August the sun may give you a better welcome than this damp mist would do. The babes seem well, only there are many little disturbing influences that torment, distract, and offend. I take it that Women have had almost too heavy a burden, the minding of babes being a heavier task than the bearing of them. Though I believe one gains much by being thrown out of thought, set to baby games and made to brush and sweep and clean the little new life blossoms. . Must they not be set in the way?

He might read, he did read, books about tortures inflicted by Eastern potentates; he heavily underscored in his copy of Young's *Night Thoughts* a line about death:

This king of terrors is the prince of peace;

he read and marked up a book published in 1887 by the Progressive Publishing Company, entitled *The Crimes of Christianity*. But also he walked every day through the fields and lanes of East Chaldon and Mappowder, observing and enjoying the common manifestations of nature. When he found a worm in the dust and hazard of the road he put it back into the grass. He did not seek company, but when the occasion arose there was not a villager who was not glad to talk with him.

It is on a basis of strength and tenderness that his unique writings are built. It is yet one more example of the wonder of true art that these writings, with all their disturbing and fascinating imaginativeness, should rest firmly on a central, poised humanity of feeling.

If I quote from Lao Tse it is not by way of offering anything like a comprehensive wisdom, still less a summing-up. There are essential characteristics of Powys that the passage does not touch. But he was fond of Lao Tse, and something of his own character in its aspect of simplicity-with-profundity, and something of his genius for the 'stillness' which 'makes muddy water clear', are well suggested in the passage:

The ancient wise men were skilful in their mysterious acquaintance with profundities.

They were fathomless in their depths; so profound, that I cannot bring them forth to my mind.

They were cautious, like one who crosses a swollen river.

They were reserved, like one who doubts his fellows.

They were watchful, like one who travels abroad.

They were retiring, like snow beneath the sun.

They were simple, like newly felled timber.

They were lowly, like the valley.

They were obscure, like muddy water.

May not a man take muddy water and make it clear by keeping still?

May not a man take a dead thing and make it alive by continuous motion?

Those who follow this Tao have no need of replenishing, and being devoid of all properties, they grow old without need of being replenished.

Powys's growing old and his death were full of quiet acceptance. If 'Lie thee down, Oddity!' reflects an attitude to man and death which may seem to put death at a premium, his writings are there to show that the tragi-comedy of the myriad myriad Oddities held the attention of his sharp, humorous, extraordinary mind, and was worth his profoundest feeling in contemplation.

# BIBLIOGRAPHY

FOLLOWING is a list of the main works of T. F. Powys. Except where otherwise indicated the publishers are Chatto and Windus. Those marked * or † were published in the United States by Viking Press and Knopf respectively.

*An Interpretation of Genesis*, privately printed 1908; distributed later by William Rider. Re-published by Chatto and Windus, 1929.*

*Soliloquies of a Hermit*, Andrew Melrose 1918; re-published by Chatto and Windus, 1929. This book was first published in New York, by Arnold Shaw in 1916, with the title *The Soliloquy of a Hermit*.

*The Left Leg*, with *Hester Dominy* and *Abraham Men*, 1923.

*Black Bryony*, 1923.†

*Mark Only*, 1924.†

*Mr. Tasker's Gods*, 1924.†

*Mockery Gap*, 1925.†

*A Stubborn Tree*, Archer, 1926.*

*Innocent Birds*, 1926.

*Feed My Swine*, Archer, 1926. Included in *The White Paternoster*.

*A Strong Girl*, Archer, 1926. Together with *The Bride*, which is included in *The White Paternoster*.

*Mr. Weston's Good Wine*, 1927.*

*The Rival Pastors*, Archer, 1927. Included in *The White Paternoster*.

*What Lack I Yet?* Archer, 1927. Included in *The White Paternoster*.

*The House with the Echo*, 1928 (Short Stories).†

*The Dewpond*, Elkin Mathews, 1928. Included in *Bottle's Path*.

*Fables*, 1929 (Title changed to *No Painted Plumage* in 1934).†

*The Key of the Field*, Chiswick Press, 1930. Included in *Bottle's Path*.

*Uriah on the Hill*, Gordon Fraser, 1930.

*Kindness in a Corner*, 1930.†

*Christ in the Cupboard*, Lahr, 1930. Included in *The White Paternoster*.

*Uncle Dottery*, Douglas Cleverdon, 1930.

*The White Paternoster*, 1930 (Short Stories).

*When Thou Wast Naked*, Golden Cockerel Press, 1931. Included in *Bottle's Path*.

*The Only Penitent*, 1931. Included in *Bottle's Path*.

*Unclay*, 1931.†

*The Tithe Barn*, K. S. Bhat, 1932. Together with *The Dove and the Eagle*, which is included in *Bottle's Path*.

*The Two Thieves*, with *God* and *In Good Earth*, 1932.†

*Make Thyself Many*, Grayson and Grayson, 1935.

*Captain Patch*, 1935 (Short Stories).

*Goat Green*, or *The Better Gift*, Golden Cockerel Press, 1937. Included in *Bottle's Path*.

*Bottle's Path*, 1946 (Short Stories).

*God's Eyes a-Twinkle*, a selection of the stories, with a preface, by Charles Prentice, 1947.

Among Powys's translated works are *Le Bon Vin de M. Weston*, Gallimard, 1950; and *Le Capitaine Patch*, Gallimard, 1952. Both these works are translated and prefaced by Henri Fluchère. There have also been editions of Powys's works in Russian, Italian and Norwegian.

Works still in manuscript include *An Interpretation of the Book of Job ; Sheep's Clothing ; Amos Lear;* and *Georgina, a Lady*. It seems that Powys himself had no very strong wish that these should be published.

I have been given some valuable information by Mrs. Sally Powys, wife of Francis Powys, about the dates of composition

of a number of T. F. Powys's writings. She found the information, written in T F.'s own hand, in his copy of Moffat's *New
Translation of the Bible.* Here it is:

*   *An Interpretation of Genesis*, 1905-1907.
    *Soliloquies of a Hermit* written during the spring of 1915.
    *Mr. Tasker's Gods:* this book was written during the winter
        of 1916 and completed the following summer.
    *Black Bryony* written in 1917—a winter book.
    *Hester Dominy*, an early story 1918.
    *The Left Leg* and *Abraham Men* written in 1921.
    *Mark Only* written during the summer and autumn of 1922.
    *Mockery Gap* commenced in the spring and completed in
        the summer of 1923.
    *Innocent Birds* written in 1923-1924 during the winter
        months.
    *House with the Echo:* then that item was written between
        the years 1917-1918 [*sic*].
    *Mr. Weston's Good Wine*, commenced January, 1924,
        ended autumn, 1925.
    *Dew Pond*, summer 1926.
    *Fables*, 1927.

In addition to the books and articles on Powys or the
Powyses referred to in the body of the present book, I am
conscious of having benefited in one way or another from
William Hunter's *Novels and Stories of T. F. Powys* (Gordon
Fraser, 1930); from a hint or two thrown out here and there
by F. R. and Q. D. Leavis; and from a thoughtful article by
R. C. Churchill (printed in *The Critic*, 1947) entitled 'The Path
of T. F. Powys'.

# ACKNOWLEDGMENTS

MY THANKS are due to all those members of the Powys family who have talked to me about Theodore, in particular Mrs. Violet Powys, Francis, Susan, and John Cowper Powys. Mr. Louis Wilkinson has likewise been most kind in giving help. Among others who have helped are Mrs. Sally Powys, Miss Phyllis Playter, and Mr. Graham Boycott. Messrs. Chatto and Windus, and of course Mrs. Powys, kindly gave permission to quote from the works ; and I have also to thank Fr. Brocard Sewell for allowing me to quote from an article by Mr. Louis Wilkinson for *The Aylesford Review*, and Miss Alyse Gregory for a quotation from her article in *The London Magazine*.

# INDEX

| DATE DUE | | | |
|---|---|---|---|
| | | | |
| | | | |
| | | | |
| | | | |
| | | | |
| | | | |
| | | | |
| | | | |
| | | | |
| | | | |
| | | | |
| | | | |
| | | | |
| | | | |
| | | | |
| | | | |
| GAYLORD | | | PRINTED IN U.S.A. |